Critical Guides to Spanish Texts

29 Gil Vicente: Casandra and Don Duardos

Critical Guides to Spanish Texts

EDITED BY J.E. VAREY AND A.D. DEYERMOND

GIL VICENTE

Casandra and Don Duardos

Thomas R. Hart

Professor of Romance Languages,
University of Oregon

Grant & Cutler Ltd *in association with*
Tamesis Books Ltd 1981

I.S.B.N. 84-499-5241-7
DEPÓSITO LEGAL: V. 3.113 - 1981

Printed in Spain by
Artes Gráficas Soler, S.A., Valencia

for

GRANT AND CUTLER LTD
11 BUCKINGHAM STREET, LONDON, W.C.2.

Contents

For Eugenio Asensio

Preface

References to the text of the *Auto de la sibila Casandra* and the *Tragicomedia de Don Duardos* are to my own edition in Clásicos Castellanos: *Gil Vicente, Obras dramáticas castellanas*, ed. Thomas R. Hart (Madrid: Espasa-Calpe, 1962).

Parenthetical references to the Bibliographical Note are given by a number in italics, followed where necessary by a page number, thus: (*11*, 40). The Bibliographical Note is extremely selective and is limited primarily to studies in English and Spanish. Some other studies are cited in footnotes.

As an Appendix I have transcribed two chapters of *Primaléon* from the unique copy of the first edition now in the Cambridge University Library so that students may compare them with Vicente's adaptation in *Don Duardos*. I am grateful to the Syndics of the Cambridge University Library for permission to include them in this volume. I have transcribed the text according to the norms used in my edition of Vicente's *Obras dramáticas castellanas*. Additions to the text are placed in square brackets: [e] *stava*. A word or letter which should be omitted is placed in parentheses: *he anda(n)do*. Any other change is indicated by italics and the original reading is given in a footnote.

I am grateful to Professor Alan Deyermond of Westfield College (University of London) for giving me the opportunity to take a fresh look at two plays which I had first written about more than twenty years before. I began work on this book while on sabbatical leave in Oxford in the spring of 1979. I should like to express my thanks to the members of the Oxford Spanish staff who discussed this project with me and especially to Professor P.E. Russell (who arranged for me to have access to the splendid Spanish and Portuguese collections of the Taylor Institution), and Mr F.W. Hodcroft. My colleague Steven F. Rendall read a first draft of much of the material and offered a number of very helpful suggestions; the final typescript was prepared for the press by the exemplary Production Editor of *Comparative Literature*, Nan Coppock-Bland.

T.R.H.

I Introduction

For the student of Spanish literature, the plays of Gil Vicente are fascinating because they both are and are not a part of that literature. The most obvious link between our two plays and the literature of Spain is of course the language itself. Vicente's choice of Castilian rather than Portuguese was surely determined in part by the fact that his sources were Castilian: the shepherds' plays of Juan del Encina and Lucas Fernández, together with the Spanish version of the romance of chivalry *Guarino mezquino*, for *Casandra*; the romance of chivalry *Primaleón* for *Don Duardos*. Yet Vicente is by no means simply an imitator of foreign models. None of the Salamancan shepherds' plays is so rich and subtle as *Casandra*, while in *Don Duardos* Vicente has taken a run-of-the-mill cnivalric romance and turned it into one of the glories of the Spanish theater. In doing so, moreover, he points out a road not taken by the later Spanish *comedia* by making it a play of character rather than one of incident.

Both *Casandra* and *Don Duardos* are typical of Vicente's theater in that they offer reworkings of material that he had already used in other plays. *Casandra* is the last of his Castilian Christmas plays and may be seen as a fuller working-out of motifs present in the first, the *Auto pastoril castellano*. In *Don Duardos*, Vicente returns to the theme of the disguised prince which he had explored in the delightful *Comedia del viudo*. Both *Casandra* and *Don Duardos* offer abundant proof of his gifts as a lyric poet, and Casandra in particular reveals his close ties to the splendid heritage of *poesía de tipo tradicional* which is shared by both Spain and Portugal. Both plays reveal his skill as a comic writer, for example in the sparkling dialogue between Casandra and Solomon or in the marvellous parody of courtly conversation which we hear from the lips of Camilote and Maimonda. Both *Casandra* and *Don Duardos* have attracted more attention from distinguished scholars— Dámaso Alonso, María Rosa Lida de Malkiel, Leo Spitzer, to name but three—than any of Vicente's other plays. While much surely

remains to be done, some essential points seem now definitively
established.

II Sources, texts, dates

Vicente took the story of his sibyl Casandra, who believes that she
is to be the mother of God, from a fifteenth-century Italian romance
of chivalry, *Guerrino il meschino*, by the Florentine Andrea da
Barberino. A Castilian version, *Guarino mezquino*, by Alonso
Hernández Alemán, was published in Seville in 1512. No copy
of this first edition has survived, but editions of 1527 and 1548
have come down to us. The book must, therefore, have been reason-
ably popular; some of those who attended the first performance
of *Casandra* would doubtless have read it.

Not everyone who read *Guarino* liked it. Juan de Valdés places
it among a group of romances of chivalry which "demás de ser
mentirosíssimos, son tan mal compuestos, assí por dezir las mentiras
muy desvergonçadas, como por tener el estilo desbaratado, que
no ay buen estómago que los pueda leer".[1] Cervantes, too, mentions
it when Don Quijote indignantly rejects the arguments of those
who question the truthfulness of the romances of chivalry: "y
también se atreverán a decir que es mentirosa la historia de Guarino
Mezquino".[2]

Mentirosa it certainly is:

Adventures and misadventures succeed each other endlessly;
duels and battles galore are fought and won; monsters are
slain, prisoners released, treacheries thwarted, and tempta-
tions withstood; journeys range to the fabulous Orient, to
the marvels of a Sibylline cavern, to Hell and to the Earthly
Paradise; and through it all Guerrino moves, upright and
unshatterable, from a nameless childhood slavery (whence
the epithet *Meschino*) to the discovery of his royal parentage,
the release of his parents from imprisonment, marriage with
the Persian princess of his heart, happy years of kingship,

---

[1] *Diálogo de la lengua*, ed. Juan M. Lope Blanch (Madrid: Castalia, 1969),
p. 168.

[2] I, p. xlix; ed. Martín de Riquer (Barcelona: Juventud, 1968), p. 496.

and a saintly death at the age of fifty-six.[3]

For his play, Vicente chose only one small portion of this vast assortment of knightly adventures. In Tunisia, Guarino hears that there is a sibyl in Italy who may be able to give him news of his parents. In Reggio Calabria, he is told that "aquí cerca está la sabia Sibila, la qual estava virgen en este mundo, y que ella creía que Dios havía de decendir en ella a encarnar, quando encarnó en Nuestra Señora la Virgen María, y que por aquesto ella se desesperó y fue juzgada por aquesta razón a pena perpetua en aquesta montaña".[4] The sibyl whom Guarino finally meets is not the one who thought that she was destined to be the mother of Christ, but she does give him quite a lot of information about sibyls and indeed about all sorts of other things. From her Guarino learns that there were ten sibyls: "La primera Sibila fue Sabá de Arabia; . . . La tercera fue llamada Astrie o Afrecia [Vicente's Africana, line 606] . . . Algunos quieren dezir que aquesta fue Casandra, fija del rey Priamo de Troya."[5]

From *Guarino mezquino*, then, Vicente may have taken not only the motif of the sibyl who believes that she is destined to be the mother of God but also the name Casandra, though the latter was surely known to him also from other sources, for example the *Crónica troyana*. The sibyl's reference to the Queen of Sheba may have given him the idea of pairing Casandra with Solomon. The connection between Sheba and Vicente's Casandra was first pointed out sixty years ago by the art historian Georgianna Goddard King, who observed that in medieval art Sheba and Solomon often appear together. Elsewhere, Solomon is found with a sibyl, for example on the main portal of the Convent of Christ at Tomar, if indeed the male figure depicted there is Solomon, as I.S. Révah believed. The portal, designed by Juan de Castillo, was completed in 1515 and we know that Gil Vicente, or at any rate *a* Gil Vicente — the identification of playwright and goldsmith has never been definitely established — was "vedor [that is, supervisor] de todas as

---

3   Ernest Hatch Wilkins, *A History of Italian Literature*, revised by Thomas
    G. Bergin (Cambridge, Mass.: Harvard Univ. Press, 1974), p. 135.

4   1527 ed., fols 67^v and 68, quoted in *9*, 184.

5   Quoted in *9*, 185.

obras . . . d'ouro e prata" at Tomar from 1509 to 1513.

Like many of Vicente's works, *Casandra* is not based on a single source. Vicente fits the materials he takes from *Guarino mezquino* into a dramatic structure adapted from the Nativity plays of the Salamancan dramatists Juan del Encina and Lucas Fernández.[6] He had already explored some of its possibilities in the *Auto pastoril castellano* and in the *Auto de los reyes magos*. In *Casandra*, as so often in Vicente's theater, we see him returning to material he had used in earlier plays and developing it along different lines. Stephen Reckert, elaborating an idea proposed by Eugenio Asensio, has argued persuasively that Vicente's is an experimental theater, an art of theme and variations made necessary by the limited resources offered him by the earlier Hispanic theater. Variation, combination, and repetition are its very essence.[7]

Don Duardos, too, is based on a romance of chivalry, this time a continuation of the famous *Palmerín de Olivia*, the anonymous *Primaleón*, published in Salamanca in 1512. This edition is known only from a single copy, now in the Cambridge University Library.[8] Like *Guarino mezquino*, *Primaleón* was popular; there were eleven editions of the Spanish text before the end of the century, as well as translations into French, English, and Italian. Many of those who read *Don Duardos* when it was new must also have known *Primaleón*. They may have regarded Vicente's play somewhat as a reader today regards a film based on a best-selling novel.

A reader familar with *Primaleón* would have found few surprises in Vicente's play, either in the plot or in the treatment of the principal characters, Don Duardos and Flérida. The two works nevertheless make quite different impressions. In part, this is because Vicente omits many incidents and precisely those most characteristic of a romance of chivalry. In part, too, it comes from the play's mood of "suave melancolía"—the phrase is Dámaso Alonso's—evoked by the measured pace of its stanzas. Because Vicente follows

---

6 A possible dramatic source is the liturgical *Ordo Prophetarum*, in several versions of which a sybil foretold the coming of Christ (*11*, 18-19; see also pp. 45-46 and plate 1 for later sixteenth-century versions).

7 "Teatro de vanguardia en el siglo XVI", in *8*, 29-59.

8 See F.J. Norton, "The first edition of *Primaleón*, Salamanca, 1512", *Bulletin of Hispanic Studies*, XXXVII (1960), 29-31.

his source so closely, a comparison of the play with the corresponding passages in *Primaleón* reveals a good deal about the way Vicente conceived his task of adapting the work for the stage and about the skill with which he accomplished it. There is unfortunately no modern edition of *Primaleón*; for the convenience of students who may wish to attempt a detailed comparison of a portion of Vicente's text with its source, I have transcribed Chapters 98 and 101 of *Primaleón* from the unique copy of the first edition now in Cambridge. (See Appendix, pp. 78-88.)

As in the case of *Casandra*, it is misleading to speak of *Don Duardos* as based on a single source. In both plays Vicente combines motifs drawn from a romance of chivalry with other material of quite a different kind. In *Don Duardos* he returns to the tradition of the *momo* or court masque. Eugenio Asensio sums up the matter very well: "*Don Duardos* salió del *Primaleón* . . . Pero la presentación escénica, el montaje, la selección de cuadros obedeció a la pauta usual de los momos."[9]

Like *Casandra*, too, *Don Duardos* shows Vicente returning to material he had already used in earlier plays. The motif of the prince who conceals his true identity in order to be near the woman he loves is touched on in the *Comédia de Rubena* and becomes central in the *Comedia del viudo*. It may be rewarding to think of *Don Duardos* as an essay in implicit self-criticism of the way similar materials are handled in *Viudo*. (Révah's assertion that *Don Duardos* is the earlier of the two plays has not been accepted by most other scholars.) There, for example, Don Rosvel reveals his identity almost immediately to Paula and Melicia though not to their father the widower, while Don Duardos keeps his identity secret until the very end of the play. We may note, too, that Don Duardos never speaks like a country bumpkin, as Don Rosvel does on his first appearance and as he continues to do whenever the *viudo* is present. In general, the comic elements are much more tightly woven into the fabric of the play in *Don Duardos* than in *Viudo*.

---

[9] "De los momos cortesanos a los autos caballerescos de Gil Vicente", in his *Estudios portugueses* (Paris: Fundação Calouste Gulbenkian, 1974), p. 36. On the *momos*, see also I.S. Révah, "Manifestations théâtrales prévicentines: les *momos* de 1500", *Bulletin d'Histoire du Théâtre Portugais*, III (1952), 91-105, and N.D. Shergold (*II*, 126-36).

Rubena, *Viudo*, and *Don Duardos* are generally believed to belong to the early 1520s. Vicente's interest in romantic comedy at this time may suggest that he had recently become acquainted with the work of Torres Naharro, whose collection of plays, the *Propalladia*, was published in Naples in 1517. I believe, however, that Révah goes too far when he asserts that *Don Duardos* is "inexplicable" without the example of Torres Naharro's *Comedia Aquilana*.[10] There is no chronological difficulty. Though the *Aquilana* is not included in the *Propalladia* of 1517–it first appears in the Naples edition of 1524–Vicente might have read it in manuscript or in an *edición suelta* (chapbook) which has not come down to us. Joseph E. Gillet suggests that it was composed around 1520.[11]

Whether or not Vicente modelled *Don Duardos* on the *Aquilana*, a comparison of the two plays may help to bring out more clearly the special qualities of his work.[12] Unlike *Don Duardos*, and unlike other plays by Torres Naharro himself, *Aquilana* contains no songs. Conversely, *Don Duardos* has no *gracioso* or *graciosa* like the saucy servants Faceto and Dileta in *Aquilana*. The scene in which Dileta humiliates Felicina (a counterpart to that in which Faceto demands payment from the King before he will reveal Aquilano's identity) is hard to justify dramatically, coming, as it does, at the very end of the play. The comic elements of Torres Naharro's play–e.g., the *juego de pullas* (a ritual exchange of insults) in Act II or the mock incantation in Act III–seem poorly integrated with the main plot, in marked contrast to *Don Duardos*. This is the more surprising in that Torres Naharro seems to have given more thought to the principles of dramatic construction than did Vicente.

Vicente surpasses Torres Naharro in the delicacy and complexity of his characterization. We know precisely what sort of man Don Duardos is, not one who would easily put up with the teasing of a Faceto, as Flérida would hardly allow herself to be humiliated by a

---

[10] "La *Comédia* dans l'œuvre de Gil Vicente", *Bulletin d'Histoire du Théâtre Portugais*, II (1951), 31.

[11] *Torres Naharro and the Drama of the Renaissance*, Vol. IV of *'Propalladia' and other works of Bartolomé de Torres Naharro*, ed. J.E. Gillet (Philadelphia: Univ. of Pennsylvania Press, 1961), p. 478.

[12] The argument of Torres Naharro's play is conveniently set out in Gillet, IV, pp. 537-45.

Dileta. Torres Naharro's characters, moreover, are static in a way that Vicente's Don Duardos and Flérida are not. It is true that Feliciana behaves differently in different parts of the play but we should hardly say that she develops. The attraction she feels toward Aquilano is explicitly sexual, appropriate in a Renaissance wedding-play but quite foreign to the spirit of *Don Duardos*. Nor is it easy to say what Aquilano sees in her, whereas Don Duardos' love for Flérida is made believable in part because we can form an idea of the qualities which draw him to her.

No manuscripts of any of Gil Vicente's works are known. For most of the plays we must rely on the *Copilaçam de todalas obras de Gil Vicente*, printed in Lisbon by João Alvarez in 1562, nearly thirty years after the death of the playwright. The *Copilaçam* of 1562 is not, however, a safe guide. A careful comparison of the one play printed in Vicente's lifetime and under his supervision, the *Auto da barca do inferno*, printed around 1518 and now preserved in a single copy in the Biblioteca Nacional in Madrid, with the same play as it appears in the *Copilaçam* reveals a good many differences. According to I.S. Révah, the differences are due solely to "the carelessness, stupidity, and bad taste" of Gil Vicente's son Luís, who prepared the *Copilaçam* for the press.[13] There are, however, other possible explanations for some of the differences between the text of the *edición suelta* and that of the *Copilaçam*. One is that Vicente himself may have made changes in his work after the appearance of the first edition; another is that some of the changes may have been introduced by the censors appointed by the Inquisition. It is nonetheless probable that most of the differences are due to the intervention of Luís Vicente and that they were introduced on his own initiative and not because of the demands of the Inquisition.[14]

No *edición suelta* of *Casandra* is known. An editor of the play has no choice but to rely on the *Copilaçam* of 1562. The case

[13] *Recherches sur les œuvres de Gil Vicente*. I. *Édition critique du premier 'Auto das barcas'* (Lisbon: n.p., 1951), p. 10; my translation.

[14] See the reviews of Révah's book by Marcel Bataillon, *Bulletin Hispanique*, LIII (1953), 206-12, and Eugenio Asensio, *Revista de Filología Española*, XXXVII (1953), 279-86.

of *Don Duardos* is very different. There is a second edition of the *Copilaçam*, printed in Lisbon by Andrés Lobato in 1586. It has long been recognized that for most of the plays this second edition simply reprints the text of the first. The many differences between the editions, when they are not simply attributable to printers' errors, are the result of changes demanded by the Inquisition. For *Don Duardos* alone, however, a comparison of the two editions reveals differences of quite a different kind, for example the inclusion in '1586' of scenes which are not found in '1562' and which are surely not the work of the ecclesiastical censors. These differences have been analyzed by Stephen Reckert, who concludes that the text of '1586' is that of a *pliego suelto* emended to satisfy the demands of the Inquisition. No copy of this is known, but we know of its existence from the list of prohibited books prepared by the Inquisition in 1551, in which the publication of the emended edition is authorized: "O auto de dom Duardos que nom tiver cēsura como foy emendado". When the *Copilaçam* of 1562 was printed, however, the Inquisition had temporarily relaxed its demands. *Don Duardos* accordingly appears there without the emendations introduced by the censors, but, like the other plays, it was subjected to the scrutiny of Luís Vicente, who introduced a number of changes, including the suppression of the fine comic scene which introduces Grimanesa (see below, pp. 68-70). Neither '1562' nor '1586' thus reproduces Vicente's own text of *Don Duardos*. In the first, the text has been mutilated by Luís Vicente; in the second, by the ecclesiastical censors. A really satisfactory edition would have to combine readings from both versions; such an edition has been announced by Reckert.[15]

There is general agreement that *Casandra* is the fourth of Vicente's Castilian plays though not about the dates of all four. The *Auto de la visitación* offers no problems: it was first performed on June 7, 1502, to celebrate the birth of Prince John, the future John III, on the morning of the previous day. The *Auto pastoril castellano* and *Auto de los reyes magos* have traditionally been held to belong to

[15] For further details on the two versions, see *8*, 236-469.

December 1502 and January 1503 respectively. (In the Clásicos Castellanos edition, the date of the latter play is incorrectly given as 1502.) Révah, however, has suggested assigning them instead to December 1509 and January 1510.[16] This would bring them closer to *Casandra*, which Révah believes was first performed in December 1513 (*9*, 190-2). Most earlier critics had assigned it to 1509.

The *Copilaçam* of 1562 gives no date for the first performance of *Don Duardos*. In the second edition of 1586 the play is preceded by a prologue addressed to King John III. A portion of this prologue is quoted below in Chapter 4, "Language and Style" (pp. 31-2). In it Vicente mentions the plays he had composed for Queen Eleanor and opposes these imperfect works to his new play, *Don Duardos*, whose "conveniente retórica" he hopes will satisfy the "delicado spíritu" of the new King. Révah reasons that *Don Duardos* must be the first play that Vicente dedicated to John III and that it must therefore date from 1522. The play's unusual length—more than 2000 lines—would be accounted for by its having been conceived as a work to be read rather than performed, and this in turn would be a consequence of the suspension of theatrical performances at court during the period of mourning for Emmanuel the Fortunate, who had died in December 1521.[17]

---

[16] I.S. Révah, "Gil Vicente", *Dicionário das literaturas portuguesa, galega e brasileira*, ed. Jacinto do Prado Coelho (Oporto: Livraria Figueirinhas, 1960), p. 865.

[17] Révah, "La *Comédia*" (see note 10, above), pp. 10-12.

III Staging

Casandra was probably staged very simply. It was first performed before the royal family and their attendants immediately after Christmas Matins, just as some of Juan del Encina's Nativity plays were first performed before the Duke and Duchess of Alba (*11*, 40). The only requirement specified in the text is a curtain which can be drawn to reveal the "discovery space" or inner stage occupied by the Virgin and her Child accompanied by four angels at the end of the play.

Don Duardos offers opportunities for a more elaborate presentation. Its subject matter offers many links with the *momos* or court pageants popular at the court of Portugal as they also were at other European courts. No doubt one reason Vicente was attracted to its source, the romance of chivalry *Primaleón*, was that he could see possibilities for treating it in terms already familiar to him from his work on the festival plays. The latter, like court masques in other countries, often appear to have been conceived primarily as vehicles for elaborate stage effects: one measure of a nobleman's wealth and liberality was his willingness to spend vast sums on a single evening's entertainment.[1]

No records of expenditures for costumes and properties, like those which throw so much light on the development of the later Spanish theater, have so far been discovered for any of Vicente's plays. Nor are there any records of payments to actors: we do not know whether the plays were performed by professional actors or by courtiers. Since Vicente often asks his actors to sing—every character who speaks in *Casandra* also sings and all except Casandra and the angels dance—some of the roles may have been played by court musicians.

The stage directions in the *Copilaçam* of 1562 are too brief to be of much help to us in our attempts to visualize the stage action.

[16] See my edition of Vicente's *Farces and Festival Plays* (Eugene: Univ. of Oregon Books, 1972), pp. 38-45.

A comparison of the *Auto da barca do inferno* in the *Copilaçam* and
in the *pliego suelto* published in Vicente's lifetime reveals that the
stage directions are sometimes greatly abridged in the *Copilaçam*.[2]
Révah is surely right in supposing that the changes are the work of
Vicente's son Luís, who prepared the text of the *Copilaçam* for the
press. A further piece of evidence is offered by *Don Duardos*. In the
Copilaçam of 1562, the stage direction which follows line 108 tells
us that after the departure of Primaleón and Don Duardos the
Empress and Flérida remain seated on the stage until Camilote
and Maimonda enter. A little later, however, Camilote proposes to
Maimonda that they should go to the Emperor's court in
Constantinople:

> A Constantinopla vamos,
> señora, al emperador
> Palmeirín. (163-5)

They must, therefore, now be somewhere else. The second edition
of 1586 resolves the difficulty; we recall that the text of *Don
Duardos* printed there was not revised by Luís Vicente. In this
edition the corresponding stage direction reads: "*Apartarse han
estas figuras, y entra Camilote y Maimonda, la más fea criatura que
nunca se vio, y Camilote loándola dize.*" The exit of the Emperor
and all his court thus marks a change of scene, as it does also after
line 422 when Don Duardos goes to seek the advice of Olimba.

As in the Elizabethan theater and in the later Spanish *comedia*,
the lines spoken by the actors often tell us where and, if necessary,
when the action takes place. It is safe to assume that Vicente's plays
were staged in the same way, without scenery and with only those
properties essential to the action. There was no curtain: one scene
flows immediately into the next, often with only a word from one
of the actors to mark the change of scene. Often, too, a change of
scene is marked simply by the departure of one group of actors
and the entrance of another. Thus, in *Don Duardos*, the scene shifts
after line 519 when Don Duardos and Olimba leave the stage and the
gardener Julián enters with his family. The audience still needs to be
told where the new scene takes place. Julián's lines do this, but they
also do much more. The *huerta*, first mentioned in line 524, is

---

2 Révah, *Recherches* (see Ch. 2, note 13), pp. 80-3.

described in detail in 545-57. These lines tell us that it is spring and, in doing so, anticipate the association of the *huerta* with its mistress, Flérida, whose spring-like beauty will soon ripen into the full summer of her love for Don Duardos. At the same time, they give Julián an opportunity to declare his love for his wife Costança Ruiz and thus to reiterate the theme of the irresistible power of love which dominates the whole play. The evocative quality of Julián's description of spring in the *huerta* does more than scenery ever could to establish a mood for the ensuing scenes.

The rapid shift from one scene to another made possible by the absence of scenery permits equally rapid shifts in tone, for example when Don Duardos' initial declaration of love for Flérida is followed immediately by the entrance of Camilote and Maimonda, whose conversation burlesques the same motif and in doing so reminds us once more that in this play it is love which guides the actions of all the principal characters.

Seventeenth-century Spanish *comedias* were performed outdoors and in broad daylight, as were Shakespeare's plays.[3] Vicente's plays were performed indoors and doubtless with some form of artificial light, but the texts suggest that no attempt was made to change the lighting to fit the needs of a particular scene. Don Duardos' first soliloquy is preceded by several references to night (798-809) and ends with the announcement that "Esto es ya claro día" (886). The playing time of the scene bears no relation to the fictional elapsed time, though no doubt some attempt was made to suggest the latter, perhaps by having Don Duardos mime the action of digging for buried treasure. He might do so before line 838 and again before 886. The central portion of the soliloquy, the long apostrophe to Flérida, would thus appear as a pause in his night's labor.

The last scene of the play is similarly introduced by Don Duardos' reference to stars in line 1927—an upward sweep of his hand would help to drive the point home—and by the ship-captain's announcement that "la noche haze escura" (1977). Finally, Artada tells us that Flérida's departure takes place "en la noche más serena/que el cielo hazer podía" (1998-9). Once again, the lines not only set the

---

3 See J.E. Varey, "The Staging of Night Scenes in the *Comedia*", *The American Hispanist*, II, 15 (February 1977), 14-16.

scene but also help to establish its emotional atmosphere: Flérida no longer attempts to resist the love that draws her to Don Duardos, a point symbolized by her falling asleep in his arms, as Artada, in the concluding *romance*, tells us that she does:

> Al son de sus dulces remos
> la princesa se adormía
> en braços de don Duardos
> que bien le pertenecía. (2042-5)

The last point would be brought out also by mime: the final stage direction tells us that the *romance* was "representado".

The mention of mime may remind us that the staging of Vicente's plays, as of any others, involves more than just scenery and lighting. We must try to imagine the play as it would be presented on stage by actors, not just read aloud before a listening audience, much less read silently and in solitude. We must suppose that in *Don Duardos* the stage direction *"Ahora se combaten los dos"* after line 72 refers to a stage fight which would have thrilled the audience by a demonstration of spectacular sword-play, as audiences today thrill to similar scenes in Shakespeare. In performance it would be easy to bring out the contrast between Flérida's indifference as she carries out her father's command to stop the fight and Don Duardos' emotional turmoil as he falls in love with her quite literally at first sight. (Though Flérida has been on stage since the beginning of the play, Don Duardos has presumably taken no notice of her; his whole attention has been directed toward the Emperor and Primaleón.)

Again, we must try to imagine the audience's surprise when it first sees Don Duardos dressed as a gardener, following Olimba's advice that he appear "vestido de paños viles" (485). It would be underscored by the marked change in Julián's attitude toward Don Duardos when he first sees him. A moment before, hearing Don Duardos' voice coming from the other side of the garden gate—that is from off stage—Julián had addressed him respectfully as "señor":

> Catad, señor, que esta entrada
> nunca se dio ni dará,
> que esta huerta es muy guardada. (576-8)

Now, on seeing him, he addresses him in a more familiar way: "Pero

¿dónde sois, hermano?" (579). The word "pero" and the question itself suggest both that Don Duardos' appearance does not match his voice and that it is itself outlandish. We may suppose, too, that during Don Duardos' next speech Julián shows himself puzzled as to how he ought to address this strange visitor. Curiosity and greed finally persuade him to disregard his orders to let no one enter the *huerta*—and to return to addressing his visitor as *vos*. The little scene is rich in comic possibilities which are only hinted at in the words of the text.

Our task is not yet done when we have tried to imagine how Vicente's lines would be spoken by actors. We must also try to imagine how they would be heard by the character to whom they are addressed, that is, we must try to imagine the gestures or facial expressions which might serve to reveal their effect upon him or her. We need, too, to think of the possibilities for purely visual effects, for example, the contrast in *Don Duardos* between the magnificent costumes of the Emperor and his court and the bizarre getup of Camilote and Maimonda. In *Primaleón*, Chapter 101 (fol. 115), Camilote and Maimonda are described as "tan feos que no havía hombre que los viesse que dellos no se espantasse". He is "alto de cuerpo y membrudo" and "todo velloso, que parescía salvaje". We may suppose that in *Don Duardos* he would have been dressed in animal skins, both to mark his distance from the courtly world of Don Duardos and Flérida and to remind the audience that he represents a literary type, the *caballero salvaje*, familiar to them from the sentimental novels popular at the time.[4]

Finally, we must not overlook the role of music. Each of the fragments of song cited by Don Duardos and Flérida (1233-51) would have been sung, not just recited, and the familiar melodies must have greatly strengthened the scene's ability to evoke the world of courtly love-talk reflected in the *cancioneros* of the period.

Révah has argued that *Don Duardos* was written in 1522, when

---

[4] The origins of the literary figure of the *caballero salvaje* —or wild man—are to be found in folklore. See Richard Bernheimer, *Wild Men in the Middle Ages* (Cambridge, Mass.: Harvard U.P., 1952); H.V. Livermore, "El caballero salvaje. Ensayo de identificación de un juglar", *Revista de Filología Española*, XXXIV (1950), 166-83; and Alan D. Deyermond, "El hombre salvaje en la novela sentimental", *Filología*, X (1964), 97-111.

theatrical performances at the Portuguese court were suspended because of the death of King Emmanuel in December 1521. The play would thus have been intended not for performance but for reading.[5] This would help to account both for the play's length and also for the difference in stylistic level which separates it from his earlier plays. If Révah's view is correct, *Don Duardos* would offer even more impressive testimony as to Vicente's profound understanding of the arts of the theater. For *Don Duardos*, even though it may have been composed for reading, reveals Vicente's constant attention to the possibilities for dramatic expression offered by costume, dance, music, and mime.

---

5   "La *Comédia*" (see Ch. 2, note 10), pp. 11-12.

IV Language and style

Only fifteen of Vicente's forty-four plays are written in his native Portuguese. Eleven are wholly in Castilian. The rest are bilingual, some characters speaking one of the two languages and some the other. We are so used to assuming that a writer will naturally choose to express himself in his mother tongue that Vicente may seem an oddity, one of that select company that includes such writers as Joseph Conrad, Samuel Beckett, and Vladimir Nabokov. But there is a most important difference. Conrad left Poland at seventeen and sailed on English ships as a merchant seaman for more than ten years before settling in England and trying to make his living as a writer in English. Beckett went to Paris soon after his graduation from Trinity College, Dublin, and has lived in France almost continuously ever since. Nabokov went to England after the Russian Revolution of 1917 and graduated from Trinity College, Cambridge, in 1923, but already as a child in Russia he had had English governesses, had read English books, poured English Golden Syrup on his Russian bread and butter, and bathed with English soap. By contrast, there is no evidence that Vicente ever set foot in Spain or that he had personal ties with anyone or anything in that country. He belongs rather to the medieval tradition in which a writer's choice of language was often governed more by questions of genre or of literary tradition than by his own nationality.[1]

In the Middle Ages Galician-Portuguese was the accepted medium for lyric poetry not only in Portugal but also in Spain. It is misleading to say, as so many handbooks do, that Castile produced no lyric poetry in the Middle Ages. The court of Alfonso el Sabio was the first important literary center in the Iberian Peninsula, though the poetry composed there was written not in Castilian but in Galician-Portuguese. Alfonso himself used the language for his *Cantigas de Santa Maria*, while the prose works produced under

[1] See Leonard Forster, *The Poet's Tongues: Multilingualism in Literature* (Cambridge: Univ. Press, 1970), Ch. 2.

his direction are in Castilian. More than two hundred years later, the Marqués de Santillana observed that "non ha mucho tienpo qualesquier dezidores e trobadores destas partes, agora fuessen castellanos, andaluzes, o de la Estremadura, todas sus obras conponían en lengua gallega o portuguesa".[2] Some of Santillana's own *canciones* are deeply indebted to the Galician-Portuguese tradition. One is written in that language, as are the earlier poems included in the mid-fifteenth century *Cancionero de Baena*.[3]

By the sixteenth century the situation had changed. Spanish poets no longer wrote in Galician-Portuguese, while almost every important Portuguese writer composed at least a part of his work in Castilian. The list includes such distinguished figures as Francisco de Sá de Miranda, Jorge de Montemayor, and Luís de Camões. Those who wrote only in Portuguese, like the dramatist António Ferreira, are the exception rather than the rule, as these lines from Diogo Bernardes' elegy for Ferreira imply:

> Pois dando à pátria tantos versos raros
> um só nunca lhe deu em língua alheia.[4]

Vicente stands apart from his compatriots only because some of his Castilian works, like Montemayor's novel *La Diana*, have earned a place among the classics of Spanish literature.

For Vicente, as for most of his Portuguese contemporaries, Castilian must have seemed the appropriate language for literary use, whether one spoke it as his mother tongue or not. They surely read books in Spanish far more often than books in Portuguese. They had little choice. Book production in Portugal in the first two decades of the sixteenth century remained on an extremely small scale. It is doubtful that as many books were printed in Portugal in this period as in a single moderately prosperous center of Spanish printing like Burgos.[5]

2   Quoted in A.D. Deyermond, *The Middle Ages* (London: Ernest Benn, and New York: Barnes and Noble, 1971), p. 20, in the series *A Literary History of Spain*, ed. R.O. Jones.

3   See Deyermond, pp. 130, 183.

4   "For, though he gave his country so many excellent verses, he never wrote one in a foreign tongue." Cited in *14*, 294.

5   See F.J. Norton, *A Descriptive Catalogue of Printing in Spain and Portugal 1501-1520* (Cambridge: Univ. Press, 1978), pp. 491-3.

Vicente's knowledge of Spanish did not, however, come exclusively from books. He would have heard the language spoken constantly at court. Relations between the courts of Spain and Portugal were extremely close. Two of the three wives of Vicente's first patron Emmanuel the Fortunate were daughters of Ferdinand and Isabella of Spain. The third was a sister of Charles V, as was the wife of Emmanuel's successor, John III. There is every reason to suppose that Vicente, like other persons closely associated with the court, had a fluent command of spoken Spanish.

We know from Francisco Delicado's *Lozana andaluza* (1528) that the language of the Spaniards then resident in Rome was heavily influenced by Italian. Many of Delicado's characters belong to the lower strata of society, but even so scrupulous a stylist as Juan de Valdés often imitated Italian idioms and borrowed freely from Italian to designate concepts for which Spanish lacked suitable terms.[6] Valdés seems to have made a deliberate effort to make his Castilian easy for Italians to understand, using, for example, *planto* (Italian *pianto*) instead of *lloro* and *demandar* (Italian *domandare*) instead of *pedir*, and declaring that "voy siempre acomodando las palabras castellanas con las italianas, y las maneras de dezir de la una lengua con las de la otra, de manera que sin apartarme del castellano sea mejor entendido del italiano" (147). Many of the Spaniards whom Vicente knew at the Portuguese court may have made a similar effort to adjust their Castilian speech for easy comprehension by Portuguese hearers.

The Spanish Vicente heard spoken by Spaniards resident in Portugal may, then, have been rather different from that which he would have heard in Spain itself. Certainly the Castilian spoken at court by Portuguese must often have been colored by the speakers' native language. We should probably not be too quick to say that it was "incorrect". Grammatical usage in Spanish was less fixed in the first decades of the sixteenth century than it is today and the same was true of Portuguese. Vicente must have felt much less pressure to speak and write Spanish "correctly" than a foreign student does today.

He may also have felt that the use of Spanish by several generations

---

[6] *Diálogo* (see Ch. 2, note 1), pp. 26-7.

of Portuguese writers authorized constructions, like the charac-
teristically Portuguese inflected infinitive, which have never existed
in Castilian. [7] Vicente's attitude may have been rather like that of
an American who feels no obligation to follow current usage in
England when speaking, or even when writing, his mother tongue.

It is hardly surprising that Vicente's Castilian often allows traces
of his native Portuguese to show through. Less often, however, than
a modern reader familiar with both languages might suppose.
Spanish and Portuguese were much more alike at the beginning of
the sixteenth century than they are today. Many of the apparent
lusismos in Vicente's Castilian, like the omission of the preposition
a before a personal object or after a verb of motion, were then
current in both languages though they survive today only in
Portuguese. There is a danger that students will censure Vicente
for using constructions which they might equally well find in
Garcilaso. Furthermore, the sixteenth-century printed editions
are not safe guides to what Vicente wrote. It is often impossible
to be certain whether an error should be attributed to Vicente
himself or to the Portuguese printers who set his works in type.
The printers' difficulties were compounded by the fact that Spanish
and Portuguese are so very similar to one another. As everyone who
has tried to learn both languages knows, the similarities are as much
a hindrance as a help. It is all too easy in speaking or writing one
of the languages to introduce words and expressions from the other.
The *Copilaçam* of 1562 abounds in errors of this kind, using, for
example, Portuguese *se* for Spanish *si* (*Don Duardos*, 594) or intro-
ducing hybrid forms like *depués* for Spanish *después* (*Casandra*,
452) on the model of Portuguese *depois*.

For Vicente's contemporaries, then, Spanish was hardly a foreign
language. Their attitude is well described by Amado Alonso:

> Hoy, sin duda alguna, vemos el portugués y el castellano como
> dos lenguas diferentes; pero es mucho lo que la divergencia de
> ambas lenguas debe al respectivo desarrollo posterior a 1600 y a
> las diferencias en la conservación y en el olvido del fondo anti-
> guo; además, la doble literatura no sólo es un importantísimo

---

[7] For an excellent discussion of "la tradición castellanizante" in Portugal,
see *1*, 136-42.

motivo para que nos aparezcan el castellano y el portugués como dos "lenguas", sino que efectivamente las dos literaturas han sido y son dos diferentes factores reales de fijación. Pero en la Edad Media *y* en el siglo XVI el sentimiento dominante debió ser que el portugués y el castellano eran dos variedades de una misma lengua, aunque con diferencias muy importantes.[8]

In Vicente's day Spaniards and Portuguese seem to have understood each other with little or no difficulty. His plays offer many examples of conversations in which one speaker uses Portuguese and the other Spanish. An example is the opening scene of *Quem tem farelos?*, in which the Portuguese servant Apariço and his Spanish counterpart Ordoño compare the shortcomings of their respective masters. Another is the conversation between the Portuguese wife Costança and her Spanish suitor Juan de Zamora in the *Auto da Índia*. Such scenes offer eloquent testimony that knowledge of Spanish in Portugal was not confined to court circles.

Nor was a knowledge of Spanish literature limited to those whose education and means gave them access to books. Even today some Spanish ballads remain alive in Portuguese oral tradition, often retaining linguistic features which give clear evidence of their Castilian origin.[9] Many traditional lyrics, too, are found in both Castilian and Portuguese versions and form part of a common literary heritage. Significantly, Vicente sometimes assigns a song in Spanish to a character who speaks in Portuguese, like Inês Pereira, whose first lines in the play which bears her name are a fragment of a Spanish song:

> Quien con veros pena y muere,
> ¿qué hará quando no os viere?

Vicente's songs reveal his profound understanding of the popular lyric traditions of both Spain and Portugal. His fondness for *poesía de tipo tradicional* links him with many Spanish dramatists of the Golden Age, most notably, of course, with Lope de Vega. Many of

---

8 Review of Dámaso Alonso's edition of *Don Duardos*, *Revista de Filología Hispánica*, IV (1942), 284.

9 See Ramón Menéndez Pidal, *Romancero hispánico (hispano-portugués, americano y sefardí): teoría e historia* (Madrid: Espasa-Calpe, 1951), II, pp. 321-9.

Vicente's songs, like some of Lope's, are not only delightful in themselves but are tightly woven into the fabric of the plays in which
they appear. As with Lope, it is often impossible to decide whether
a particular song is Vicente's own creation or one that he has taken
from popular tradition, perhaps with changes to adapt it to its new
dramatic function.

   In most cases, as C.M. Bowra observes, "Vicente's lyrics belong to
the dramatic action and do something for it".[10] What that something is has been admirably analysed by Eugenio Asensio, who
identifies three principal functions for the songs in Vicente's plays
(*3*, 164-7). The first is to establish a setting for the action. Song
then accompanied many of the activities of daily life, as it still does,
though to a rapidly diminishing degree, in rural communities in
Spain and Portugal. (When a shepherd can carry a transistor radio to
the fields with him, as some of them now do, the survival of traditional songs and, indeed, of other forms of traditional behavior is
obviously threatened.) In *Casandra*, four angels lull the infant Jesus
to sleep by singing (655-71). Solomon leaves Casandra with her
aunts the sibyls and goes to the village in search of his uncles Moses,
Abraham, and Isaiah. They return singing a *serranilla* (313-21),
perhaps intended to symbolize the lapse of time necessary for
Solomon's journey to the village and back. The second function
Asensio assigns to Vicente's songs is that of defining the social
status or personality of the singer. Casandra's first song, "Dicen
que me case yo", is an excellent example. The third is to duplicate
the dramatic action on an epic or lyric plane. An example cited by
Asensio is the *romance* which brings *Don Duardos* to a close.

   Vicente's songs, of course, were meant to be sung, not just read
silently. Some familiarity with the music of the period can help us
imagine the effect of Vicente's plays in performance. We should
remember, too, that many of the songs were accompanied by dance
and some of them by mime. The final stage direction of *Don
Duardos*, in the *Copilaçam* of 1562, reads, "Este romance se disse
representado, e depois tornado a cantar por despedida" (fol. 137;
my italics).

---

[10] "The Songs of Gil Vicente", in his *Inspiration and Poetry* (London:
Macmillan, 1955), p. 91.

I.S. Révah has noted that "the most superficial reading [of *Casandra*] reveals an astonishing sense of construction, a construction, moreover, which is not simply theatrical but also plastic and musical. The entrances and exits of the characters are determined by the needs of dance and song" (*9*, 168; my translation). The musical needs to which Révah refers are those imposed by the elaborate polyphonic settings fashionable in the court music of the period. Settings of this kind were often given to lyrics and melodies taken from popular tradition (*2*, 51-2). Asensio has noted that Vicente often assigns his songs to four characters or to a multiple of four, surely because the musical setting demanded four voices (*3*, 154-5). In *Casandra*, Solomon and the sibyls enter dancing and presumably also singing a *chacota* (stage direction before line 220); Solomon and the prophets sing and dance (313-21); four angels sing a lullaby to the Christ Child (655-71); all the characters—eight, or, if they are joined by the angels, twelve voices—sing the final call to arms. The use of polyphonic settings for lyrics which are closely linked to the popular tradition may be seen as symbolizing the fusion of courtly and popular elements which characterizes so much of Vicente's theater.

The balance between the two components is, of course, not the same in all his plays. *Casandra* stresses popular elements, *Don Duardos* courtly ones. The difference may correspond to different stages in Vicente's career. He himself seems to have been aware that *Don Duardos* marks a departure from his earlier work as a playwright. In the *Copilaçam* of 1586 the play is preceded by an important prologue omitted in the first edition of 1562. In it Vicente addresses his new patron John III in the following terms:

Como quiera (excelente Príncipe y Rey muy poderoso) que las comedias, farças y moralidades que he compuesto en servicio de la Reina vuestra tía (quanto en caso de amores) fueron figuras baxas, en las quales no había conveniente retórica que pudiesse satisfazer al delicado spíritu de V[uestra] A[lteza], conocí que me cumplía meter más velas a mi pobre fusta. Y assí con desseo de ganar su contentamiento, hallé lo que en estremo desseava, que fue Don Duardos y Flérida, que son tan altas figuras como su historia recuenta, con *tan dulce retórica y escogido estilo* quanto se puede alcançar en

la humana inteligencia: lo que yo aquí hiziera si pudiera
tanto como la mitad del desseo que de servir a V[uestra]
A[lteza] tengo. (*8*, 261; my italics)

Samuel Butler remarks wittily in *Hudibras* that "all a rhetorician's
rules/Teach nothing but to name his tools". Wittily but perhaps
unjustly: there is good reason to believe that training in formal
rhetoric made medieval and Renaissance writers and their readers
aware of the resources of language and made them delight in seeing
those resources skillfully exploited. But Butler is certainly justified
in poking fun at the wealth of names used to designate the rhetorician's tools. The rhetorical figures were—and are—called by a bewil-
dering variety of names, most of them known today only to a handful
of specialists. On the one hand, a single rhetorical device might be
called by more than one name; on the other, different rhetoricians
often used the same term to refer to different devices. One discussion which may have been known to Vicente is the eighth chapter
of Juan del Encina's *Arte de trobar*, included in his *Cancionero*
of 1496.[11] Encina's treatment, however, is too brief to afford a
fully satisfactory basis for analyzing Vicente's text. I shall use his
terminology and shall add one of the terms used by modern rhetoricians to denote the same figure.[12]

The figure Encina calls *reiterado*, that is, the repetition of the
same word at the beginning of successive clauses or lines of verse,
may be exemplified by Flérida's words of reproach to Don Duardos:

> *En todo* quanto desseo,
> *en todo* os hallo duro
> hasta aquí.
> *Todo* siento, *todo* veo,
> y *todo* se haze escuro
> para mí. (1932-7)

The insistent repetition of a single word—we should now call it
anaphora—suggests the heightened emotional tension which Flérida
experiences at this moment. A less obvious device, which a modern

---

[11] My quotations are from Encina's *Obras completas*, ed. Ana M. Rambaldo,
I (Madrid: Espasa-Calpe, 1978).

[12] A very helpful guide is Richard A. Lanham, *A Handlist of Rhetorical Terms*
(Berkeley: Univ. of California Press, 1968).

reader may fail to notice, is that her first use of the word *todo* in line 1932 echoes Don Duardos' use of the same word to end the preceding line:

> mis dolores, mis querellas
> vencen todo. (1930-1)

Encina calls this figure *encadenado*: "Ay una gala de trobar que se llama encadenado, que en el consonante que acaba el un pie, en aquél comiença el otro" (28). Encina's example makes clear what he has in mind:

> Soy contento ser *cativo*,
> *cativo* en vuestro *poder*,
> *poder* dichoso ser *bivo*,
> *bivo* con mi mal *esquivo*,
> *esquivo* no de querer. (my italics)

A modern student of rhetoric might call this anadiplosis, the repetition of the last word of a clause or line of verse to begin the next; its use in *cancionero* poetry goes back ultimately to the *coblas capfinidas* of the Provençal troubadours.

Encina's definition of *redoblado* also leaves something to be desired, but his example shows that he refers to what a modern rhetorician would call polyptoton, the repetition of words from the same root but with different endings or prefixes. Here are some examples from Don Duardos' second soliloquy:

> Pues *acuérdesete*, Amor,
> que *recuerdes* mi señora
> que se *acuerde*
> que no duerme mi dolor,
> ni *soledad sola* una hora
> se me pierde. (1091-6)
> Porque, Amor, yo quiero ver,
> pues que *dios* eres llamado
> *divinal*,
> si tu *divinal* poder
> hará subir en borcado
> este sayal. (1103-8)

Like troubles, rhetorical figures rarely come singly. This brief passage offers several examples of alliteration (*duerme: dolor*,

soledad: sola, dios: divinal: divinal). The whole passage is an apostrophe to Love, while the last two lines are built on a metaphor in
which clothing stands for social rank, as it often does in this play.

It may be helpful to point out a few of the rhetorical features of
Don Duardos' first soliloquy. It begins with an apostrophe to the
palace where Flérida lives, *consagrado* (827) because it shelters one
whom Don Duardos will repeatedly call his God. The *tesoro* of line
829 is, of course, Flérida herself, a point made explicitly in lines
888-9; the repetition of the metaphor thus links the beginning and
end of the soliloquy. Since the palace holds such a treasure, it ought
really to be constructed of precious materials, the gold, rubies, and
emeralds of lines 832-4. The underlying rhetorical figure is metonymy, of the type sometimes called "container for the thing con-
tained". The mention of *serafines* in line 835 returns to the theme
of Flérida's divinity, which will be developed in the polyptoton of
lines 838-41 and reiterated in the religious terms—*diesa*, *devoción*,
romería—of lines 869-72. The seraphim are Flérida's ladies in waiting,
who wait upon her as the angels wait in attendance upon God. Since
Flérida is a god or goddess—Don Duardos uses the terms interchange-
ably in referring to her—it is appropriate that he should adore her,
as he does in the anaphoric "A ti adoro" of lines 844 and 847. The
contrast between Don Duardos' impassioned love for Flérida and her
apparent indifference toward him is brought out by the combination
of antithesis and polyptoton in lines 874-7:

Tú *duermes*, yo me *desvelo*;
y también está *dormida*
mi esperança.
Yo solo, señora, *velo*.

Don Duardos' hope of acceptance is given a brief life of its own in
the personification of lines 875-6, though paradoxically this is done
only to assert that his hope is asleep and thus unaware of its own
life. It is, in short, a restatement of the notion, dear to the courtly
tradition, that the lover's state is one of death in life. The soliloquy
ends with another reference to Flérida's divinity, the assertion that
God's power is shown by the fact that He has been able to create
one so wonderful (889-91). The lines may recall Calisto's first words
in *La Celestina*: "En esto veo, Melibea, la grandeza de Dios ... En
dar poder a natura que de tan perfecta hermosura te dotasse ...."

There is nothing new about either the form or the content of Don Duardos' soliloquy. The striking thing about it is that no one is there to hear him and this, of course, is a guarantee of his sincerity. Only a few moments earlier Amandria had assured Flérida that love, or more precisely talk of love, is merely a game, one every courtier must learn to play. But, as John Stevens reminds us:

> All social life is in some sense a fiction, a "game". We act many parts; and we try to act consistently, not mixing our roles . . . These fictions, which are all simplifications, are necessary; they allow social life . . . to be carried on. Nor should it be thought that they are always a burden to those who have to adopt them. Far from it. They may provide us with a refuge and release from our more complicated selves; they may give us an outlet, a channel, a form, for certain emotions and desires; and lastly, if they are habitual, they will permanently simplify our responses. (*13*, 154)

Elsewhere Stevens observes that courtly society rests upon the fiction that everyone is in love. If one wishes to be accepted in such a society, one must, in Stevens' phrase, "act the Lover". This is what Amandria believes that Don Duardos is doing, but our quotation from Stevens may help us to see that he is also doing something more. Love is a game, to be played deliberately and skillfully according to well established rules, but it is a game which permanently alters the nature of the players.

Stevens adds that "the importance of talk in the aristocratic, ideal world of courtly living can hardly be exaggerated" (159). Such talk must be learned; it is Don Duardos' talk of love which makes Flérida and her ladies in waiting suspect that he is not the simple gardener he pretends to be. The "dulce retórica y escogido estilo" to which Vicente proudly lays claim in the prologue to *Don Duardos* may represent an idealized version of the way people really spoke in the courtly society known to Vicente's first audiences.[13] Stevens observes that in the teaching of rhetoric little distinction was made between speech and writing: "Both obeyed

---

[13] Cf. A.D. Deyermond, *The Petrarchan Sources of 'La Celestina'* (London: Oxford Univ. Press, 1961), p. 100: "We must remember that anyone in Calisto's position would have been educated in the rhetorical tradition of the time, and that rhetorical devices would be used in polite speech."

the same basic rules, and served the same basic ends—to 'praise'
and to 'persuade' " (160). Stevens' formula, to praise and to persuade, offers an admirably concise way of describing the aims of
Don Duardos' conversations with Flérida.

Rhetorical figures, of course, were not found only in courtly
speech. Many features of ordinary conversation today may be
described in terms drawn from traditional rhetoric. Phrases like
"¡Buena la hemos hecho!" ("A fine mess we've made of it!") or
"¡Para canciones estoy yo!" ("I'm in no mood for songs!") may
be seen as examples of irony and, if spoken in certain circumstances,
of litotes or understatement. We should not be surprised to find
such figures in *Casandra*. The end of Casandra's opening monologue:

¡Y piensan que ser casada
que es alguna buena estrena! (21-2)

may be classified as an example of apodioxis, which Lanham defines
as "rejecting an argument indignantly as impertinent or absurdly
false". The rime *hecha: prehecha* in Moses' account of the Creation
(lines 356-7) is an example of polyptoton. Margit Frenk Alatorre
cites a number of examples of the latter from folksongs and it would
be easy to find examples of many other figures.[14] It remains true
nevertheless that such figures occur more frequently and in more
elaborate forms in courtly than in popular poetry. The stylistic
difference between *Casandra* and *Don Duardos* remains marked
despite the fact that many of the same rhetorical figures are found
in both plays.

---

14 *Entre folklore y literatura* (Mexico City: El Colegio de México, 1971), p. 61.

V Imagery

The American poet Wallace Stevens observes in one of his aphorisms that "reality is a cliché from which we escape by metaphor".[1] For Stevens, as for most modern poets, a successful image must be new, surprising: a fresh statement of a uniquely personal impression or judgment. Medieval and Renaissance poets conceived imagery very differently. They were not primarily concerned with expressing a personal view of the world, one meant to interest the reader precisely because of its difference from other, more familiar views. The values and beliefs expressed in their poetry are not private and personal; they are those generally accepted in their society. The poet's task is not to give meaning to the world but to discover the meaning God has embodied in it, and his images are means to that end. They will be much less concerned with the precise rendering of vivid sensory experiences than with the moral judgments implied by the things described. "The minds of both writers and readers", asserts Rosemond Tuve, "had long been accustomed to seeing a network of analogies in the world of external nature . . . The transitory rose, the triumphant worm in the grave . . . –the 'particulars' in Elizabethan poems turn into metaphors at a touch."[2] Vicente's images work in just this way.

We may begin with one of the "particulars" mentioned by Tuve, the rose. In *Casandra* Cimeria reports that in her vision of the Virgin and her child the angels address Mary as "rosa florida" (481). Mary, of course, is not literally a rose and it would not be quite accurate to say that she is called one simply because of her physical beauty. It is rather that a relationship is being proposed between the moral excellence of the woman and the beauty of the flower. As the rose is superior to other flowers, so Mary is superior to all other women. The association of Mary with the rose and with other

[1] *Opus posthumous* (New York: Alfred A. Knopf, 1957), p. 179.

[2] *Elizabethan and Metaphysical Imagery* (1947; rpt. Chicago: Univ. of Chicago Press, 1963), p. 161.

flowers recurs throughout the play. Isaiah declares that:

> lirios, flores y rosas ·
> muy preciosas
> procuran de semejalla. (555-7)

Peresica calls her "la cerrada flor parida" (691); finally, Isaiah hails
her with the words "ave, rosa, blanca flor" (764), where the color
white symbolizes virginity. None of these images is new; they go
back to the assertion of the bride in the Song of Songs, traditionally
associated with Mary, that "I am the rose of Sharon, and the lily of
the valleys" (Canticles ii.1).

Casandra, too, calls herself a flower:

> No será ni es nacido
> tal para ser mi marido;
> y pues que tengo sabido
> que la flor yo me la so,
> dizen que me case yo:
> no quiero marido, no. (214-19)

She means that she is in a class by herself, *la flor y nata*, the cream
of the crop. The phrase itself is innocent enough. It is found in a
number of *poesías de tipo tradicional*, like this one from Juan
Vásquez' *Villancicos y canciones* (1551):

> Que yo, mi madre, yo
> que la flor de la villa m'era yo.

> Ibame yo, mi madre,
> y todos me decían "¡Garrida!"
> m'era yo.
> Que la flor de la villa m'era yo.[3]

But the image also suggests other, darker possibilities, which were to
be exploited a century later by Góngora in a famous *letrilla*,
"Aprended, flores, de mí". Flowers may symbolize the brevity of
human life, as in the familiar lines from Isaiah (xl.6): "All flesh is
grass, and all the goodliness thereof is as the flower of the field."
Still more to the point, in the light of Casandra's refusal to marry,
is this passage from Sebastián de Covarrubias' *Tesoro de la lengua*

---

[3] Cited, with other versions, in Daniel Devoto, ed., *Cancionero llamado
"Flor de la rosa"* (Buenos Aires: Losada, 1950), p. 105.

castellana o española of 1611: "Flor, en la donzella, se dize la vir-
ginidad y entereza, que como flor que está asida a su mata o rama,
está lustrosa, alegre y rutilante; en cortándola luego se marchita. De
do se dixo desflorar, corromper la donzella."[4]

The same image appears later in the prophets' song "Sañosa está
la niña", where Casandra is said to be "hermosa como las flores"
(317). The song anticipates the later contrast between Casandra
and Mary and suggests that Casandra's outward beauty belies her
inward pride: if she is "hermosa como las flores", she is also "sañosa
como la mar". She is thus unlike Mary, whose beauty is the outward
manifestation of her spiritual excellence. One important theme of
the play can be summed up as the transformation of Casandra from
one who wants only Mary's status as the virgin who will bear a child
to one who aspires to be like Mary in every possible way.

At the beginning of the play, Casandra appears perfectly content
to live apart from those she considers her inferiors, "n'esta sierra a
mi soltura" (203). At the end she abandons her self-imposed isolation to become a member of the *militia Christi*, the army of
Christian believers. She is now ready to accept Paul's exhortation to
become "a good soldier of Jesus Christ" (II Timothy ii.3). The
theme of the Church militant is prepared by a whole series of images
earlier in the play. In line 717, for example, Solomon addresses the
child Jesus with the phrase *"ab eterno* capitán". Earlier still, Cimeria
had said that Mary is:

> contra Lucifer *armada*,
> con virgen *arnés* guardada,
> ataviada
> de *malla* de sancta vida.
>   Con leda cara y *guerrera,*
> plazentera,
> el resplandor piadoso,
> el *yelmo* todo humildoso. (466-72)

These images, too, are traditional. Paul urges his readers to "put on
the armor of light" (Romans xiii.12) and to "put on the whole
armor of God" (Ephesians vi.11). Elsewhere he speaks of "the
helmet of salvation" (Ephesians vi.17) and of putting on "for a helmet,
the hope of salvation" (I Thessalonians v.8). Finally, the song "Muy

[4]   Ed. Martín de Riquer (Barcelona: Horta, 1943), p. 601, s.v. *flor.*

graciosa es la doncella" asserts, surprisingly for a modern reader, that Mary's beauty surpasses that of warfare itself, an excellent illustration that for Renaissance poets imagery is concerned much less with the accurate rendering of sensory experience than with moral values and meanings:

> Digas tú, el cavallero
> que las armas vestías,
> si el cavallo o las armas
> o la guerra es tan bella. (774-7)

The pervasive military imagery makes it difficult for me to agree with those who see the final call to arms as having nothing to do with the rest of the play.[5]

Don Duardos, too, is built upon a few recurrent images. None of them would seem new to a reader familiar with the poetry of the fifteenth-century *cancioneros* and with the *poesía de tipo tradicional*.[6] Vicente's contribution lies in the skill with which he has used these traditional images to keep his audience's attention— not necessarily, of course, their conscious attention—fixed on the principal themes of his play. The most important of these images is that of the garden, the *huerta*, which becomes, in Dámaso Alonso's words, "un personaje mudo, que está en las mentes y en los corazones de todos" (*1, 22*). The association of an enclosed garden with an unmarried girl is very old. We find it in the Song of Songs: "A garden inclosed is my sister, my spouse" (Canticles iv.12). It is common in Spanish popular tradition, as in the proverb "Niña y viña, peral y habar, malo es de guardar", and in songs like this parallelistic one from Mosen Pedro Vallés' *Libro de refranes* (Zaragoza, 1549):

> No entréis en huerto ajeno,
> que os dirá mal su dueño;
> no entréis en herto vedado,
> que [os] dirá mal su amo.[7]

5 Révah, for example, sees the song as reflecting the threat of a Moorish attack on the recently conquered city of Azemmour (*9*, 192).

6 I use this term to include both genuine folksongs, transmitted orally from generation to generation, and works by individual poets composed in the same style.

7 Cited by Margit Frenk Alatorre, *Lírica hispánica de tipo popular* (Mexico City: Universidad Nacional Autónoma de México, 1966), p. 52.

Equally traditional is the lovers' meeting in a garden. *Don Duardos* may be seen, on one level, as an expansion of one of the many songs like this from the *Cancionero musical de Palacio*:

> Dentro en el vergel
> moriré.
> Dentro en el rrosal
> matarm'an.

> Yo m'iva, mi madre,
> las rrosas coger.
> Hallé mis amores
> dentro en el vergel.
> Dentro en el rrosal
> matarm'an.[8]

In *Don Duardos*, the *huerta* is constantly associated with Flérida. Indeed, it comes, by a kind of metonymy, to represent Flérida herself. Julián counters Don Duardos' request to be admitted to the garden by answering that:

> esta entrada
> nunca se dio ni dará,
> que esta huerta es muy guardada. (576-8)

The identification of the garden with its mistress becomes even clearer when Don Duardos tells Artada that:

> Señora, soy singular
> hortelano;
> mas esta tierra es tan fuerte,
> que pienso que el trabajar
> será en vano. (965-9)

A striking use of the garden image is found at the beginning of Don Duardos' second soliloquy:

> ¡Oh, floresta de dolores,
> árboles dulces, floridos,
> inmortales:
> secárades vuessas flores
> si tuviérades sentidos
> humanales! (1079-84)

8 Ed. José Romeu Figueras (Barcelona: Consejo Superior de Investigaciones Científicas, 1965), no. 366 (pp. 444-5).

On one level this may be taken as a kind of pathetic fallacy, the kind sometimes referred to as "nature at variance".[9] Don Duardos is surprised that the leaves do not wither, as they surely would if they were aware of his emotional state. At the same time, given the repeated association of the *huerta* with Flérida herself, the lines reveal his anguish that she has thus far shown him no sign of sympathy. They amount to an accusation that her treatment of him reveals a lack of human feeling, natural enough in trees but hardly becoming in a woman.

The same figure is developed at greater length in a later soliloquy, this time one spoken by Flérida:

> ¡Quán alegres y contentos
> estos árboles están!
>   En esto veo
> que no son graves tromentos
> los que sufre Julián
>   con desseo:
> que en la cámara a do estó
> veo llorar las figuras
>   de los paños
> del dolor que siento yo,
> y aquí crecen las verduras
>   con los daños.
> Y mis jardines, texidos
> con seda de oro tirado,
>   se amustiaron,
> porque mis tristes gemidos,
> teñidos de mi cuidado,
>   los tocaron:
> y yo veo aquí las flores
> y las aguas perenales
>   y lo ál,
> tan agenas de dolores
> como yo llena de males
>   por mi mal. (1636-59)

9   See Bernard F. Dick, "Ancient Pastoral and the Pathetic Fallacy", *Comparative Literature*, XX (1968), 30.

She contrasts the indifference of the natural world represented by the garden with the sympathy of the gardens depicted on the tapestries which adorn her room in the palace. The contrast underscores the conflicting emotions within her as her growing love for Don Duardos struggles with her knowledge that he is separated from her by an unbridgeable social gulf.

The image of the garden is linked with the equally traditional one of the fire of love when Artada tells Don Duardos that she has heard Flérida say:

> que ha de mandar quemar
>   luego la huerta;
> y no ha aquí de venir,
> a ver si puede olvidar
>   esta puerta. (1505-9)

Later the same thought is expressed by Flérida herself:

> Vámonos d'aquí, Artada,
> de esta huerta sin consuelo
>   para nos,
> ¡de fuego seas quemada,
> y sea rayo del cielo,
>   plega a Dios! (1762-7)

In the *romance* which ends the play, Artada tells us that Flérida:

> en la huerta de su padre
> a los árboles dezía:

[Flérida]
> Quedaos adiós, mis flores,
> mi gloria que ser solía:
> voyme a tierras estrangeras,
> pues ventura allá me guía. (2002-7)

In her farewell to the *huerta* Flérida also takes leave of the life she has known in her father's palace; she now sets forth on the long journey to England, where she will begin a new life with Don Duardos (*15*, 5).

Don Duardos persuades Julián to admit him to the garden by telling him that it contains buried treasure and offering to share it with him. The treasure is Flérida herself, a point made by Don Duardos at the beginning of his first soliloquy:

> ¡Oh, palacio consagrado!

> pues que tienes en tu mano
> tal tesoro,
> devieras de ser labrado
> de otro metal más ufano
> que no oro. (826-31)

The same point is made even more explicitly near the end of the soliloquy:

> Darles he de este tesoro,
> porque el mío
> es Flérida, señora mía. (887-9)

Elsewhere the association is only implicit, for example when Don Duardos says to Costanza Ruiz:

> No hablemos en comer:
> dexadme gastar la vida
> en mi tesoro. (910-12)

Don Duardos intends Costanza to understand *tesoro* as referring to the treasure supposedly buried in the garden, but it is clear that he is really thinking of Flérida. So, too, when he tells Julián that:

> Nunca tan triste me vi.
> No me hallo en esta tierra,
> y este tesoro me tiene;
> éste sólo me da guerra. (1327-30)

The true meaning of Don Duardos' words is underscored by the fact that Julián accepts them at face value and takes the opportunity to suggest that Don Duardos would do well to marry a local peasant girl, Grimanesa.

Most, perhaps all, of the images Vicente uses in *Don Duardos* are found also in his source, the romance of chivalry *Primaleón*. The treasure as a metaphor for Flérida herself is no exception:

> —Ay, amigo—dezía la hortelana. ¡Quán bien andantes somos en conoceros, que de pobres y mezquinos nos havéis fecho ricos!
>
> —Muy más lo seréis—dezía Julián—que aún yo tengo de cobrar otro mayor tesoro que el que havéis visto.
>
> Y esto dezía él por Flérida, que tenía esperança de sacalla y llevándola llevar a ellos con ella porque no recibies[s]en daño y fazelles gran bien. (Ch. 123, fol. 120ᵛ)

The image is appropriate since Don Duardos can win Flérida only through his own efforts, just as digging up the treasure demands physical effort. *Primaleón* lays even more stress on the effort involved: "el cavar no lo sabía él fazer" (Ch. 97, fol. 91). In the romance, as in the play, Don Duardos' labors may be seen as a literal enactment of one of the key metaphors of the courtly tradition, the lover's service as an act of homage to his lady.

The images do not stand alone. Each is used by a specific person and in a specific situation. But they need also to be seen in their relationship to the play as a whole. One important function of the imagery is to link the separate scenes, to recall earlier scenes and foreshadow those still to come—in short, to ensure that the audience's attention is not allowed to wander from the central concerns of the play. Though most of the imagery in *Don Duardos* comes from *Primaleón*, its function in the two works is quite different. In part, this is simply because the account of Don Duardos' adventures in the romance is a great deal longer than in Vicente's play. A given image, even if it occurs a number of times, will be less striking in the romance than in Vicente's much shorter version for the stage. Verse calls attention to the language of the text in a way prose does not, while in a theatrical performance the actors may emphasize key images by voice and gesture.

In building Don Duardos' declarations of love on a few frequently repeated images, Vicente underscores the obsessive quality which it shares with the love poetry of the *cancioneros*. The *cancioneros*, too, offer many examples of love as warfare and as an all-consuming fire, images which recur throughout Vicente's play. I have pointed out elsewhere that in *Don Duardos* Vicente "gives new life to the time-worn conventions of courtly love, precisely by insisting that they *are* usually conventions and then going on to show that, in this special case, we are not concerned with conventions at all but with deeply felt emotions".[10] Don Duardos' first soliloquy, spoken alone in the garden at night, comes almost immediately after the scene in which Artada warns Flérida of the insincerity of courtly lovers:

Es un modo de hablar

[10] "Courtly Love in Gil Vicente's *Don Duardos*", *Romance Notes*, II (1960-61), 105.

> general, que oís dezir
> a amadores . . .
> Si alguno al dios Apolo
> hiziesse adoración
> por su dama,
> y esto estando solo
> y llorando su passión,
> éste ama. (774-6, 786-91)

Don Duardos' soliloquy reveals the uniqueness of his love for Flérida
by showing that in his mouth the familiar words are still charged
with meaning; they are not spoken merely to persuade Flérida to
accept his love.

The quality of Don Duardos' love for Flérida does not set him
apart from all the other characters in the play. Vicente often suggests
that two characters are experiencing the same sort of emotion by
having them use the same images. As Flérida's love for Don Duardos
grows, she comes more and more to speak the same sort of language
he does. Thus, Don Duardos' impassioned statement "ardo en fuego"
(743) is countered by Flérida's curt rejoinder:

> Deves hablar como vistes,
> o vestir como respondes. (744-5)

At this point Flérida is hardly aware of Don Duardos as an individual. She sees him only as a member of a different social class who
has no right to address her in these terms. Later, however, Flérida
will confess to Artada that "Ardo en fuego de contino" (1825). As
the sincerity of Don Duardos' protestations of love is guaranteed by
their presence in a soliloquy, so the sincerity of Flérida's confession
is assured by the fact that it is addressed to Artada and not to Don
Duardos himself.

The imagery also links Don Duardos with another figure, the
grotesque *caballero salvaje* Camilote. Don Duardos repeatedly refers
to Flérida as "mi dios" (1515) and speaks of her "[ojos] divinos"
and "manos divinales" (755). In the same way, Camilote tells
Maimonda that:

> Por vos cantó Salamón
> el cantar de los cantares
> namorados, (115-17)

thus implicitly linking her with Mary and, incidentally, suggesting that she is no longer young, a point made more explicitly elsewhere (218-31). Camilote insists that:

> no está
> 'n el mundo muger divina
> sino ésta (244-6)

and that when he first saw her "Vi a Dios" (315). All this, of course, is thoroughly conventional, as the plural *enamorados* in the subtitle of the *Celestina* of 1501 reminds us: "compuesta en reprensión de *los locos enamorados*, que . . . a sus amigas llaman e dizen ser su dios".[11] In assigning this familiar conceit to both Don Duardos and Camilote, Vicente stresses the central theme of his play, the irresistible power of love, most explicitly stated near the end of the play in Artada's song:

> Al Amor y a la Fortuna
> no hay defensión ninguna. (1950-1)

Significantly, the phrase is proverbial; Gonzalo Correas cites it in the form "Amor i fortuna, no tiene defensa alguna".[12]

Artada's couplet reminds us that Vicente's imagery can hardly be separated from his gift for capturing one of the principal themes in a memorable line or two. Often, as in this case, the line will be traditional—a proverb or a fragment of a popular song—but given a new force and concreteness by its connection with the specific action of the play. Every reader will have his own favorites. Mine would include Don Duardos' assertion that:

> Por lo impossible andamos:
> no por ál. (1113-14)

Another is his statement that "perdí de ser quien solía" (1723). Once more, Vicente's line recalls the *poesía de tipo tradicional*; one may compare it with these from the *Silva de varios romances* (Barcelona, 1561):

> No soy yo quien ser solía,
> no, no, no,

---

[11] See "The Deification of Women" in Gillet, *Torres Naharro* (see Ch. 2, note 11), pp. 337-44.

[12] *Vocabulario de refranes y frases proverbiales (1627)*, ed. Louis Combet (Bordeaux: Féret, 1967), p. 76.

sombra soy del que murió.[13]

In the play, however, the line gains in intensity because of the special situation of Don Duardos. He is no longer the person he was both because he is pretending to be the gardener's son and because he has been transformed by his love for Flérida. Moreover, on one level the line may be seen as a deliberate attempt to tantalize Flérida by suggesting that he is not what he seems, and thus a sign that he is beginning to despair of ever persuading her to accept him on his own terms. The line comes just before his most impassioned appeal to her, just before he will reveal his true identity by killing Camilote. Here, as often in *Don Duardos*, Vicente gives triumphant expression to points that are indeed present also in *Primaleón* but which are never summed up so splendidly in the rambling prose of the romance.

---

[13] Ed. Antonio Rodríguez-Moñino (Valencia: Castalia, 1953), p. 182. The *glosa–culta*, in this case—shows that this is a love song.

VI Characterization: Casandra

A.A. Parker has observed that the Spanish *comedia* of the seventeenth century is "essentially a drama of action and not of characterization ... The plot and not the characters is the primary thing" (7, 3-4). Our two early sixteenth-century plays by Gil Vicente work rather differently. Dámaso Alonso has contrasted the "lenta matización psicológica" in Vicente's treatment of Don Duardos and Flérida with "los cambios bruscos e infundamentados del teatro de Lope", suggesting that "aquí, en la expresión, por matices sumamente delicados y pequeños, de las variaciones de un alma es donde está el mayor valor dramático de la *Tragicomedia*" (*1*, 26). The "lenta matización psicológica" which Alonso finds in *Don Duardos* is perhaps unique to that play. It may have something to do with the sheer length of the text—more than 2,000 lines—which was perhaps written to be read rather than performed before an audience.[1] But in *Casandra*, too, though in a rather different way, character is more important than action. The action arises out of the character of Casandra and is shaped by the special kind of person she is.

In *Casandra*, as in the earlier *Auto pastoril castellano* and *Auto de los reyes magos*, Vicente centers his attention not on the Nativity itself but rather on its effect on those who witnessed it, or, more precisely, on its effect on the protagonist whose attitude toward it is different from that of his or her fellows. Different at least at the beginning of the play. The birth of Christ inaugurates a new era in human society; the play will end by composing the differences which earlier had separated the protagonist from the other characters. In *Casandra*, however, this structure is turned upside down. Casandra, unlike Gil and Gregorio in the earlier Christmas plays, cuts herself off from her society because she is less, not more, ready than the other characters to accept the message of the Incarnation. As a result, the end of the play leaves her much more radically trans-

[1] See Ch. 2, p. 18.

formed than her counterparts in the other shepherds' plays.

Like Vicente's earlier Christmas plays, *Casandra* begins with a soliloquy by the protagonist. From it we learn two things, first that she does not wish to marry, and second that she is proud. If she will not marry, it is because she is convinced that there is no man who is worthy of her:

> Pues séame Dios testigo
> que yo digo
> que no me quiero casar.
> ¿Quál será pastor nacido
> tan polido
> ahotas que me meresca? (5-9)

To marry, Casandra insists, means for a woman losing her liberty, "su libertad cautivando" (15). Aubrey Bell saw Casandra's attack on marriage as a reflection of "the sad life of married women in Portugal".[2] More recently, Melveena McKendrick has argued that *Casandra* is "the first [Spanish play] in which the theme of active feminism appears. The figures of the unrequited or importunate lover and the unyielding maiden are common in the early drama but the rejection of man by maid is born not of principle but of personal preference. Vicente's *Auto* offers us the first, and for many years the only, example of the heroine who denounces the very concept of marriage" (6, 45). McKendrick's feminist reading of the play offers a number of interesting insights. She suggests, for example, that "Casandra has what today would be called a neurotic obsession about marriage" (49) and that "she lacks confidence in her ability to cope with life and comes to see herself as the passive object of glory" (50). I believe, however, that the play may be better understood in the light of some widespread sixteenth-century ideas on marriage.

For a convenient statement of them, we may turn to Fray Hernando de Talavera, the first Archbishop of Granada and a member of the triumvirate to whom Ferdinand and Isabella, in 1492, entrusted the administration of the newly reconquered city. In the third chapter of his treatise *De cómo se ha de ordenar el tiempo para que sea bien expendido*, Fray Hernando tells Doña María

---

[2] *Portuguese Literature* (Oxford: Clarendon Press, 1922), p. 114.

Pacheco that:

> aún devéis mirar, noble señora, que no sois libre para hacer vuestra voluntad; ca el día que fuistes ayuntada al marido en el estado matrimonial, ese día perdiste vuestra libertad. Porque no solamente tomó el marido el señorío de vuestro cuerpo, como vos tomastes del suyo, mas sois subjeta a él y obligada a vos conformar con su voluntad en todo lo que no fuere pecado mortal o venial . . . era cosa natural y mucho razonable que la mujer, que comúnmente, como tiene flaco el cuerpo y mucho menor el esfuerzo, así no tiene tan complida discreción, siga y obedesca el seso y querer del varón, que en todo es más perfecto; ca es ley general que todas las cosas inferiores e menores sean movidas por las superiores e mayores, como lo son los hombres por los buenos ángeles, e los elementos y cosas elementadas por los cuerpos celestiales.[3]

As the last sentence makes clear, the wife's subjection to her husband is only a special case of what C.S. Lewis has called "the Hierarchical conception". He explains it thus:

> According to this conception degrees of value are objectively present in the universe. Everything except God has some natural superior; everything except unformed matter has some natural inferior. The goodness, happiness, and dignity of every being consists in obeying its natural superior and ruling its natural inferiors. When it fails in either part of this twofold task we have disease or monstrosity in the scheme of things until the peccant being is either destroyed or corrected. One or the other it will certainly be; for by stepping out of its place in the system (whether it step up like a rebellious angel or down like an uxorious husband) it has made the very nature of things its enemy. It cannot succeed.[4]

To those who saw or read Vicente's play when it was new, Casandra's refusal to marry must have seemed simply another manifestation of her overweening pride, a refusal to submit to any authority whatever.

---

[3] *Escritores místicos españoles*, I, Nueva Biblioteca de Autores Españoles, XVI (Madrid: Bailly-Baillière, 1911), p. 97. I have slightly modernized the text.

[4] *A Preface to 'Paradise Lost'* (1942; rpt. London: Oxford Univ. Press, 1959), p. 72.

Casandra makes her attitude perfectly clear in lines 91-3:
>   No quiero ser desposada
> ni casada,
> ni monja ni ermitaña.

The same point is later made even more explicitly in Pedro de
Luxán's *Coloquios matrimoniales*; first published in 1550, the book
had reached its eleventh edition by 1589. Near the beginning of the
first *Coloquio*, we find the following passage:

Dorotea. —Me parece que te veo agora más fresca y hermosa
que nunca te vi.

Eulalia. —Por dicha harálo los pocos cuidados que debo tener.

Dorotea. —Como no eres casada.

Eulalia. —Ni aun lo querría ser.

Dorotea. —¿Por qué causa no quieres tomar el yugo del
matrimonio?

Eulalia. —Algunas veces he sido requerida por mis padres
que me case y no lo he querido hacer.

Dorotea. —¿Por qué?

Eulalia. —Porque no querría casarme.

Dorotea. —¿Meterte monja?

Eulalia. —Ni querría ser monja.

Dorotea. —¿Por qué?

Eulalia. —Por no estar contino encerrada debajo de siete
llaves.

Dorotea. —¿Pues qué piensas de hacer, no queriendo tomar
estado ninguno: conviene a saber de ser casada o
monja?

Eulalia. —Vivir acá en el mundo, sin tener superior a quien
dar cuenta, ni aun a quien contentar.

Dorotea. —No te acabo de entender.[5]

Dorotea finds Eulalia's attitude incomprehensible, just as Cervantes
makes Grisóstomo's friends refuse to accept Marcela's assertion
that "tengo libre condición y no gusto de sujetarme".[6] Vicente's

---

5   *Coloquios matrimoniales* (Madrid: Atlas, 1943), p. 8. See Marcel Bataillon,
    Erasmo y España, trans. Antonio Alatorre (Mexico City: Fondo de Cultura
    Económica, 1950), II, pp. 255-7.

6   *Don Quixote*, I, xiv (see Ch. 2, note 2), p. 132. See Thomas R. Hart and
    Steven F. Rendall, "Rhetoric and Persuasion in Marcela's Address to the
    Shepherds", *Hispanic Review*, XLVI (1978), 296-7.

contemporaries would doubtless have felt the same way about Casandra's refusal to *tomar estado*, which strikes at the very foundations of a hierarchically structured universe.

Casandra's refusal to accept a place within the established social hierarchy is stressed repeatedly. The opposition between Casandra and "the others" is apparent in the very first words she speaks in the play:

> ¿Quién mete ninguno andar
> ni porfiar
> en casamientos comigo? (1-3)

It is stressed again in her first song, where the opposition between Casandra and those who wish her to marry is emphasized by the rhyme *yo: no*, by the repetition of the negative particle *no*, and by the emphatic position of *yo* after the verb: "Dizen que me case yo:/ no quiero marido, no" (200-1). It is, of course, still further emphasized by the fact that this couplet serves as an *estribillo*, repeated at the end of each of the following stanzas.

Casandra apparently feels no need of company. She lives alone; we learn later that her mother is dead, when Cimeria reminds her that "Tu madre en su testamiento/ . . . manda que cases" (226-8). Casandra's address to her mother in her song "Madre, no seré casada" (208) should not be attributed to carelessness on Vicente's part. It is simply a part of the traditional rhetoric of folk song, sometimes used, as here, where it is not strictly applicable.[7]

Casandra's insistence on living apart from society is underscored by the imagery. Thus, in her song "Dizen que me case yo" she asserts that "Más quiero bivir segura/'n esta sierra a mi soltura" (202-3). *Sierra* implies a lofty place from which she can look down on those she considers her inferiors—we recall the arrogant questions she asks in her opening soliloquy:

> ¿Quál será pastor nacido
> tan polido
> ahotas que me meresca?

[7] Margit Frenk Alatorre, in the Introduction to her edition of the *Cancionero de galanes* (Valencia: Castalia, 1952), observes that "en ciertos giros se nota el desgaste de las fórmulas tradicionales: [por ejemplo] el 'madre' del verso 9 [of the song "Aunque me vedes/morenica en el agua"], que está fuera de lugar, puesto que la muchacha está hablando justamente de la madre" (p. xlv).

¿Alguno hay que me paresca
en cuerpo, vista y sentido? (7-11)

Morally, however, Casandra's *sierra* is anything but *segura*, since it
symbolizes the pride which governs all her actions. The image is
repeated in the song "Sañosa está la niña", sung by Solomon and
his uncles when they join him in attempting to persuade Casandra
to marry him:

En la sierra anda la niña
su ganado a repastar,
hermosa como las flores,
sañosa como la mar. (315-18)

Here there are doubtless echoes of the *serranillas*, the Hispanic
counterpart of the *pastourelles* found in other medieval Romance
literatures. The line "sañosa como la mar" presents Casandra as a
natural force which, like the sea, is not easily subjected to man's
will. The image may have been suggested to Vicente by an idiomatic
use of the verb *ensoberbecerse* to refer to a stormy sea; Casandra
implicitly applies the word to Solomon earlier in the play (128).[8]

Casandra's self-imposed isolation, repeatedly stressed in the text,
is also brought out by the stage action. In the greater part of the
play, this isolation takes the form of an active opposition between
Casandra and the others, centering on her refusal to marry Solomon.
Almost every line is either spoken by Casandra herself or addressed
to her. The only exceptions are the prophets' song (313-21) and the
brief conversation between Solomon and the sibyls which precedes
it (296-312). Even here, however, the subject remains Casandra
herself. Part of the comic force of the latter scene lies, as Mia
Gerhardt has remarked, in the way Solomon and his aunts, their
patience exhausted, end by speaking of Casandra as if she were not
present.[9] There is a marked change after Casandra reveals her
conviction that she is to be the mother of the Messiah. Now
Abraham, Isaiah, and Solomon all reproach her for her presumption
and call her mad; Casandra confidently replies that "Aún en mi
seso estó:/que soy yo" (533-4). She will say nothing more for

8 Covarrubias, *Tesoro* (see Ch. 5, note 4), s.v. *sobervia*, says that "dezimos
del mar ensobervecerse quando está tempestuoso y agitado de los vientos".

9 *La Pastorale: essai d'analyse littéraire* (Assen: Van Gorcum, 1950), p. 144.

some 200 lines, a quarter of the play. Instead, she remains on stage, a silent witness to the prophecies of the other characters; they, in turn, address each other and pay no further attention to her. Finally, Casandra approaches the other characters and, like them, kneels before Mary and her child in adoration. To stage the scene in this way would underscore the movement of the action from Casandra's total isolation as a result of her refusal to *tomar estado* toward her final incorporation as a full member of the community of Christian believers. We may say of Vicente, as Victor Dixon says of Lope, that he "has in mind . . . the total effect of his play in the theater; . . . he seeks to communicate not only via the ear, through what is said (or sung), but via the eye, through what is presented".[10]

Alternatively, we can say that Casandra moves from a position in which she is the precise opposite of Mary to one in which she will accept Mary as a model—a movement, of course, which would also be symbolized by the stage action just discussed. Isaiah tells her that:

> Tú eres de ella al revés
> si bien ves,
> porque tú eres humosa,
> sobervia, y presumptuosa,

while Mary

> . . . humildosa ha de nascer,
> y humildosa conceber,
> y humildosa ha de criar. (538-41, 546-8)

Isaiah's speech opposing Casandra to Mary is perhaps best understood in terms of the analysis of pride offered by St Thomas Aquinas:

Pride is the opposite of humility, which . . . regards the submissiveness of man to God. And so pride . . . consists in the lack of that submissiveness, in that a person spurns the condition appointed for him by divine rule or measure, in defiance of the lesson of St Paul, *But we will not glory beyond our measure, but according to the measure of the rule that God has measured for us* [II Corinthians x.13] . . . There is always a conflict between pride and loving God, for a proud person

10 "The Symbolism of *Peribáñez*", *Bulletin of Hispanic Studies*, XLIII (1966), 11.

does not submit himself as he ought to the divine rule. Sometimes, also, it is contrary to loving our neighbour, as when we
inordinately set ourselves above him and refuse to defer to him.
This, too, derogates from divine governance which has established orders among men carrying with them duties of
respect and obligation.[11]

I suggest, then, that for a sixteenth-century reader, Casandra's
refusal to heed her aunts' advice and accept Solomon as her husband
may well have seemed a manifestation of the sin of pride, quite
apart from her mistaken belief that she is to be the mother of the
Messiah.

Vicente's treatment of Solomon helps to bring out the precise
nature of Casandra's pride. Solomon enters confidently with the
greeting "Dios te mantenga!" which Lazarillo's master was to find
so offensive. Vicente and his audience were surely aware of its
rustic flavor; its Portuguese equivalent "Deus mantenha!" seems
also to have been used by uneducated country people (*14*, 48).
Casandra does not reply. Solomon himself is compelled to speak the
welcome she refuses to offer: "y yo venga/también mucho nora-
buena!" (24-5). The point could easily be emphasized by having him
pause before line 24 to await her reply. Solomon plows bravely on,
though Casandra's stubborn refusal to show that she understands the
purpose of his visit causes him to become almost incoherent as he
tries to explain why he has come. His next lines,

> Pues te veo tan serena,
> nuestra estrena
> ya por mí no se detenga, (26-8)

echo the end of Casandra's opening monologue:

> ¡Y piensan que ser casada
> que es alguna buena estrena! (21-2)

The lines reveal Solomon's own pride; he apparently believes that it
is he who has finally made up his mind to marry Casandra, though
she makes it very clear that she has refused him before:

> lo que te dixe hasta aquí

11 *Summa theologiae*, 2a2ae.162.5, trans. Thomas Gilby, O.P. (Blackfriars in
    conjunction with McGraw-Hill Book Co., New York, and Eyre and
    Spottiswoode, London, 1972), XLIV, 135-7. Subsequent references
    will appear in my text.

> será ansí,
>
> aunque sepa de morir. (59-61)

At the same time they reveal that Solomon is totally unaware of Casandra's emotional state: at this moment she is hardly serene.

Casandra still says nothing. Solomon, increasingly unsure of himself—we may imagine that his next speech is punctuated by long pauses as he waits for her to give him some sign of encouragement—makes still another attempt to propose to her. His speech is in sharp contrast to the assurance of Casandra's opening monologue. It is not surprising that her response, the first words she speaks to him in the play, should be a blunt "No te entiendo" (34).

Solomon, however, is undaunted. He launches into a recital of his own good qualities, which leaves him a bit ashamed of having to repeat his offer of marriage to someone who so obviously fails to see him for what he is:

> Bien se ve
> que soy yo para valer
> tal, que juro a mi poder
> que, de no ser,
> ni esta paja me dé.
> Yo soy bien aparentado
> y abastado,
> valiente zagal polido,
> y aun estoy medio corrido
> de haver acá llegado. (46-55)

He concludes with a peremptory command, "Anda, si quieres venir", which Casandra just as curtly rejects: "Sin mentir,/tú estás fuera de ti"(56-8).

Solomon, like Casandra, is proud, but his pride is of a quite different kind. Casandra is proud of a distinction which, as she will learn in the course of the play, is not destined ever to be hers. Her pride strikes both at the foundations of the social order, in her refusal either to marry or to become a nun, and at her relationship to God, since she arrogates to herself a distinction which could be hers only if it were given her by God. Aquinas tells us that "pride, *superbia*, is so named because thereby a man's will aims above, *supra*, what he really is; hence Isidore notes that a man is said to be proud because he wills to appear higher than he is" (2a2ae.162.1; p. 119).

Solomon's pride, by contrast, does not touch the hierarchical principle itself. Moreover, we may assume that he really does have the things he says he has. Indeed, much of the comedy in his first scene with Casandra comes from his obvious pride in possessions which might be those of any moderately prosperous farmer (thirty-two hens). The comedy would be still further enhanced if, like María Rosa Lida de Malkiel, we believe that Solomon is dressed as a king rather than as a shepherd (*5*, 53-4). A different view is held by Duncan Moir, who believes that Solomon and the other prophets are dressed as shepherds or farmers.[12] The audience would learn Solomon's identity only when he contrasts his proverbial wisdom with Casandra's foolishness:

> tú loca, yo Salamón,
> dame razón:
> ¿qué vida fora la nuestra? (530-2)

But arguments from the presumed theatrical effectiveness of the two alternatives are hardly convincing; too much depends on the expectations of Vicente's first audiences, the conventions with which they were familiar. Though the rubric given in the *Copilaçam* is clearly wrong about either the date or the place of the first performance, and possibly about both, it is nevertheless reasonable to assume that the play was indeed first produced in a royal chapel and on Christmas Day. The spectators must surely have been expecting to see an *auto de navidad*; they must, that is, have expected to find a connection between the apparently secular scenes which begin the play and what they knew would be its ending, the news of the birth of Christ. Certainly Solomon's pride in his rustic possessions will be funnier to someone who knows that he is not just a shepherd but a king, and indeed that he is the "king Solomon [who] exceeded all the kings of the earth for riches and for wisdom" (I Kings x.23). But the costume he wears will hardly settle the matter. Even if we accept Lida de Malkiel's view that Vicente's sibyls and prophets would have worn costumes similar to those worn by such figures in late medieval art, the spectators would still have seen Solomon only as an Old Testament figure; it is hard to see what attribute he could

---

[12] Edward M. Wilson and Duncan Moir, *The Golden Age: Drama, 1492-1700*, in *A Literary History of Spain*, ed. R.O. Jones (London: Ernest Benn, and New York: Barnes and Noble, 1971). pp. 9-10.

be given that would reveal immediately who he is.

The question is further complicated by the fact that in Vicente's day there was more than one tradition connected with Solomon. As Lida de Malkiel remarks, "Salamón, cantor de la Virgen y figura de Cristo, es también ejemplo vitando del sabio que por lascivia cae en idolatría" (5, 56). Vicente himself presents Solomon in more than one way. In *Casandra*, he appears as "cantor de la Virgen" in lines which echo the Song of Songs (583 ff.), as he does also in the *Auto pastoril castellano* (343-61) and in the *Auto dos Mistérios da Virgem*, more usually known as the *Auto da Mofina Mendes*.[13] Elsewhere, however, Vicente treats Solomon quite differently. In the *Nau d'amores*, Amor asks:

> Pues ¿cómo serán sentidos
> mis poderes quántos son,
> sino en los sabios vencidos?
> Los más sabios, más perdidos,
> como os dirá Salamón.[14]

Here Vicente must have in mind the King Solomon of I Kings xi.3-4 who "had seven hundred wives, princesses, and three hundred concubines: and his wives turned away his heart . . . after other gods". Again, in the *Frágua de amor*, Vicente presents Solomon neither as "cantor de la Virgen" nor as "ejemplo vitando del sabio que por lascivia cae en idolatría" but rather as a model of wisdom:

> y dizen que a Salamón
> ni Dios ni la natureza
> no le dio más prefeción.[15]

The wise King Solomon is frequently presented in medieval art as an old man, but in *Casandra* Solomon must still be young. Casandra's aunts call him a *zagal* (220, 267).[16] Moses addresses him as "buen garçón" (584).

---

[13] *Copilaçam*, fol. 21ᵛ; *Obras completas*, ed. Marques Braga (Lisbon: Sá da Costa, 1953), I, 136.

[14] *Copilaçam*, fol. 148; ed. Braga, IV, 74.

[15] *Copilaçam*, fol. 151ᵛ; *Farces*, ed. Hart (see Ch. 3, note 1), lines 41-43.

[16] Covarrubias, *Tesoro* (see Ch. 5, note 4), s.v. *çagal*, tells us that "quedó la costumbre en las aldeas de llamar çagales a los barbiponientes, y çagalas a las moças donzellas".

More importantly, the dramatic point of the scene would be lost
if there were some obvious reason, such as a great difference in age,
for Casandra to refuse Solomon's proposal of marriage. Her later
statement to her aunts that Solomon seems to her "Ni bien ni mal"
(221) is doubtless to be taken at face value. She does not want to
hurt his feelings, if only because she has no desire to prolong her
conversation with him:

> No tomes de esto passión
> ni alteración,
> pues que no desprecio a ti. (108-10)

She is quite willing to flatter him if it will help to win him over to
her point of view: " ... pues eres cuerdo y sientes,/para mientes"
(147-8). At the same time, she is obviously irritated at his smug
assumption that any girl would be proud to have him as her husband.
Her list of the "malinas/condiciones de maridos" begins with those
who are "ensobervecidos" (126-8)—doubtless intentionally, given
Solomon's attitude in this scene, but of course also ironic in view
of Casandra's own *superbia*. Earlier Solomon had suggested that if
Casandra is unwilling to become his wife it can only be because
she is in love with someone else:

> Según el tu no querer,
> a mi ver,
> otro amor tienes allá. (88-90)

Now Casandra continues her list of unsatisfactory husbands with
those who are:

> ... llenos de mil celos
> y recelos,
> siempre aguzando cuchillos,
> sospechosos, amarillos (131-4)

and those who go:

> pavonando tras garcetas,
> sin dexar blancas ni prietas,
> y reprietas. (138-40)

The last point is especially funny if we remember that the biblical
King Solomon "loved many foreign women" (I Kings xi.1).

Neither Solomon nor any of the other characters, with the obvious exception of Casandra, learns anything new in the course of
the play. They simply see their prophecies confirmed, as they had

always known they would be. Casandra, of course, does learn something new. She learns not only that she is not the Virgin who will bear a child but that her prophecy was wrongly focused. Unlike the other sibyls, she has centered her attention on the Virgin Birth itself, saying nothing about the character of the child who will be born. God, moreover, hardly enters Casandra's prophecy at all; if she is to be the chosen Virgin, it is because she deserves to be, not because He has chosen her for special favor.

Casandra's new knowledge destroys forever the pride in her own uniqueness which had been her dominant trait at the beginning of the play. She now knows the folly of her confident assertion that "tengo sabido/que la flor yo me la so" (216-17), for she can measure the distance between herself and Mary, who is called "rosa florida" (481) and "blanca flor" (764). Her earlier confidence in her own judgement—"Aún en mi seso estó/que soy yo" (533-4)—now gives way to her recognition that:

> . . . nunca di passada
> concertada,
> ni deviera ser nacida. (737-9)

Now she can praise Mary as "corona de las mugeres" (742) and implore her intercession. Once the very opposite of Mary, as Isaiah had told her, she will presumably now try to make her own life an *imitatio Mariae*. The question of whether or not she will marry Solomon is left unresolved because it no longer matters. The important thing is that Casandra now accepts her own subordinate place in the hierarchical order. Whether she marries Solomon or not, she will surely no longer refuse to *tomar estado*, but will take her place as a faithful member of the *militia Christi*. We may assume that she joins the other characters in singing the spirited call to arms which brings the play to a close:

> Pues los ángeles sagrados
> a socorro son en tierra,
> ¡a la guerra! (784-6)

Casandra's isolation, at first a source of pleasure to her—"Más quiero bivir segura/'n esta sierra a mi soltura" (202-3)—becomes intolerable when it is no longer sustained by the firm conviction that she is superior to everyone else. One may see her as embodying A.A. Parker's conception of poetic justice in the later *comedia*.

He observes that "the degree of frustration which a character meets with at the end of a play is the measure of the dramatist's condemnation of his action, and therefore a pointer to the interpretation of the theme" (7, 8). Yet the *Auto de la sibila Casandra* does not end unhappily. When the play ends Casandra can see the folly of her own earlier presumption. It is not so much that her plans have been frustrated as that she herself has come to reject them as unworthy of the person she now aspires to be.

Casandra is not a tragedy but a comedy. Northrop Frye, in his influential book *Anatomy of Criticism*, makes a number of points which are helpful in understanding Vicente's play. "The movement of comedy", Frye asserts, "is usually a movement from one kind of society to another."[17] Comedy tends "to include as many people as possible in its final society: the blocking characters are more often reconciled or converted than simply repudiated" (165). The "blocking character" in our play is, of course, Casandra herself. Her refusal to marry Solomon and, by extension, to accept her place in the hierarchical order, is the central theme of the play. Her state is that which Frye calls "ritual bondage", in this case her obsession with the idea that she is the Virgin who will bear a child.

Frye argues that "the action of comedy ... is not unlike the action of a lawsuit, in which plaintiff and defendant construct different versions of the same situation, one finally being judged as real and the other as illusory ... A little pamphlet called the *Tractatus Coislinianus*, closely related to Aristotle's *Poetics*, which sets down all the essential facts about comedy in about a page and a half, divides [it] into two parts, opinion (*pistis*) and proof (*gnosis*)" (166). In Vicente's play, the "opinions" are the conflicting prophecies of the Virgin Birth offered by Casandra and by the other characters; the "proof" is the appearance of Mary and her child at the end of the play. Finally, Frye notes that:

> the movement from *pistis* to *gnosis* ... is fundamentally, as the Greek words suggest, a movement from illusion to reality ..., generally manipulated by a twist in the plot ...
>
> The manipulation of plot does not always involve metamorphosis of character, but there is no violation of comic

17 *Anatomy of Criticism: Four Essays* (Princeton: Univ. Press, 1957), p. 163. Subsequent references will appear in my text.

decorum when it does. Unlikely conversions, miraculous transformations, and providential assistance are inseparable from comedy. Further, whatever emerges is supposed to be there for good: if the curmudgeon becomes lovable, we understand that he will not immediately relapse again into his ritual habit. (169-71)

So, too, we must accept the humility of Casandra's last speech in the play (734-9) as marking a permanent change in her character.

In giving his *auto* a comic structure Vicente, of course, follows the pattern found in his own earlier Christmas plays and in those of Juan del Encina and Lucas Fernández. As John Brotherton has observed, "Comedy pervades [the Nativity plays]; it is their very essence, manifesting itself not only in humor, through the antics of the *Pastor-Bobo*, but also in their structure. In [them] we witness the movement from consternation to contentment, from ignorance to enlightenment, from sin to salvation."[18] In the *Auto de la sibila Casandra*, Gil Vicente goes further than his Salamancan predecessors, and further than he himself had gone in his earlier shepherds' plays, to turn this traditional comic structure into a fully developed comedy of character centering on the unique figure of Casandra herself.

---

[18] *The 'Pastor-Bobo' in the Spanish Theatre before the Time of Lope de Vega* (London: Tamesis, 1975), p. 2.

VII From 'Primaleón' to 'Don Duardos'

Everyone knows that the publication of *Don Quixote*, Part I, in 1605 destroyed the popularity of the romances of chivalry. Like so many other things that everyone knows, this one is at best a half-truth. Attacks on the romances were frequent throughout the sixteenth century, often, as in the *Quixote*, on the ground that they were not true to life. By the end of the century the publication of new ones had slowed almost to a halt.[1]

The romances of chivalry were, however, still at the height of their popularity in the 1520s when Vicente wrote *Don Duardos*. Surely they were not always taken seriously even then. Many readers must have regarded them with the amused condescension now given to the James Bond books and films. And this last point may serve to remind us that while Cervantes may have destroyed the romances of chivalry, romance itself is still very much alive, not only in the Bond books but in works of serious literature like *Moby Dick* and Henry James's *The American*.[2] James himself points to the distinction between romance and novel when he asserts that the former is distinguished by "the kind of experience with which it deals—experience liberated, . . . exempt from the conditions that we normally know to attach to it".[3] That kind of experience, specifically those forms of it which Stevens refers to as "the idealized sexual relationship which we call romantic love" and "the idealized integrity which we call honor" (21), is the subject both of *Don Duardos* and of Vicente's point of departure, the romance of chivalry *Primaleón*. One way of describing the changes Vicente made in adapting *Primaleón* would be to say that he transformed it from a

[1] Henry Thomas, *Spanish and Portuguese Romances of Chivalry* (Cambridge: Univ. Press, 1920), p. 147.

[2] Both are cited as examples of romance by John Stevens in his fine book *Medieval Romance* (London: Hutchinson, 1973; New York: Norton, 1974), p. 16.

[3] Preface to the New York Edition of *The American*, cited by Stevens, p. 17.

romance of chivalry into a romance in a more general and perhaps more fundamental sense.

The romances of chivalry are full of marvels: dragons, giants, magic potions, and, of course, knights who repeatedly triumph over the most extraordinary difficulties. Cervantes' parody of the romances in *Don Quixote* gives a clear picture of their principal features; it is easy to see why they were so often attacked as *mentirosos*. This charge can hardly be brought against *Don Duardos*. Though almost every incident in *Don Duardos* comes from *Primaleón*, the romance contains a great many incidents that Vicente omits. A prose version of *Don Duardos* would be much more like a *novela sentimental* than like a *libro de caballerías*. We should not be too quick to assume that Vicente disapproved of the marvellous elements in the romances of chivalry, either on moral grounds, like some of his contemporaries, or on aesthetic ones, like Cervantes three-quarters of a century later. It is far more likely that he simply considered them ill adapted to the kind of play he wanted to write in *Don Duardos*. Elsewhere he shows no hesitation about using them, for example, in the *Comédia sobra a divisa da cidade de Coimbra*.[4]

The chivalric elements Vicente retains in *Don Duardos* would hardly have seemed so farfetched to his contemporaries as they do to us. Only a few years before, knights errant had wandered the roads of Europe in search of adventure. Jousts, *pasos de armas*, tournaments had existed in real life, not just in books.[5] Maxime Chevalier has argued persuasively that most readers of the romances of chivalry were aristocrats, who saw in them a society like that in which they themselves lived or would have liked to live.[6] The idea

---

[4] See Alice R. Clemente, "*Comédia sobra a divisa da cidade de Coimbra*: fantasía caballeresca", in *Homenaje al Prof. William L. Fichter* (Madrid: Castalia, 1971), pp. 161-74.

[5] See Martín de Riquer, *Vida caballeresca en la España del siglo XV* (Madrid: Real Academia Española, 1965) and his essay "Cervantes y la caballeresca" in *Suma cervantina*, ed. J.B. Avalle-Arce and E.C. Riley (London: Tamesis, 1973), pp. 274-9. See also J.N. Hillgarth, *The Spanish Kingdoms 1250-1516*, II (Oxford: Univ. Press, 1978), pp. 59-63.

[6] "El público de las novelas de caballerías", in his *Lectura y lectores en la España del siglo XVI y XVII* (Madrid: Ediciones Turner, 1976), pp. 65-103. See also Daniel Eisenberg, "Who Read the Romances of Chivalry?", *Kentucky Romance Quarterly*, XX (1973), 209-33.

would hardly have seemed strange to Vicente's contemporaries. One of the more thoughtful of them, the humanist Juan Luis Vives, says much the same thing in his *Formación de la mujer cristiana*: "¿Qué placer puede hallarse en la narración de unas aventuras que tan neciamente fingen y donde mienten tan descaradamente? . . . Porque las más de las veces la causa de alabar tales libros es que en ellos contemplan como en un espejo sus propias costumbres y huélganse de que le sean aprobadas."[7] The Portuguese court for which Vicente wrote doubtless shared these tastes of their Spanish contemporaries; we have already noted that most of the books they read came from Spain and were written in Spanish.

The fantastic adventures which play so large a part in *Primaleón* are subordinated in Vicente's play to the development of the love-relationship between Don Duardos and Flérida. In stressing the romantic rather than the chivalric elements of his source, Vicente surely had in mind the tastes of his courtly audience. Just as the romances of chivalry reflect attitudes and ideals which governed the behaviour of men and women in the real world, so, too, the literature of courtly love is a reflection of a certain kind of social life. "Courtly love", writes John Stevens, "provided the aristocracy not only with a philosophy and a psychology of love but also with a code of moral behaviour. It was a school of manners, of 'politeness', of 'chere of court'. In this code—social philosophy, one might call it—the sexual attraction between man and woman was the central motif, or (to change the metaphor) the 'ground' on which everything stood. Even if you were not a lover, you must—at least in mixed company—*act the lover*" (*13*, 151). Courtly love is as much a matter of attitudes and behaviour as of literature. Stevens calls it a game, "a good Middle English term with a wealth of association: fun; a diversion; amorous play, a contest; an intrigue; the chase; the quarry. All these related meanings are apt when we are trying to reconstruct the social fiction which was courtly love in action." It is this notion of love as game that Artada has in mind when she explains to Flérida that a lover's declarations are not to be taken too seriously:

> que a todos veréis quexar,

---

[7] Cited in *4*, 139.

> y ninguno veréis morir
> por amores. (777-9)

These lines may remind an English-speaking reader of Rosalind's
assertion that "Men have died from time to time, and worms have
eaten them, but not for love" (*As You Like It*, IV.i). Yet at the
very moment she says this Rosalind is passionately in love with
Orlando and ecstatically happy at the knowledge that he loves her.
Clearly, the game of love can be played with the utmost seriousness,
so seriously, indeed, that it may even seem inappropriate to call it
a game. This is, of course, the case with Don Duardos. The point
is driven home by his first soliloquy, which comes almost immediately after Artada's speech.

How did Vicente set about adapting *Primaleón*? We may imagine
that he sketched out, perhaps only in his imagination, the portions
of the book he wanted to use for his play, then went back and re-
read them before writing the corresponding scenes. A hint that Vicente
worked in this way is perhaps to be found in Don Duardos' answer
when Flérida asks him how he came to possess the enchanted cup:

> Flérida.   ¿Dónde la huviste, Julián?
> D.Duardos.   En unas luchas reales
>   la gané. (1018-20)

The reference to *luchas* may have been suggested by the corresponding passage in *Primaleón*:

> —Ruégote, amigo Julián—dixo la infanta—que me digas
> quién te la dio.
> —Yo vos lo diré, mi señora—dixo Julián—pues vos me lo
> mandáis.
> . . . —Yo estuve en una villa adonde era señor un noble
> cavallero que tenía una fija muy fermosa y por la su gran
> fermosura se casó con ella un cavallero de alta guisa y a las
> bodas de ellos fueron fechas grandes fiestas y el cavallero,
> padre de la novia, puso tres joyas muy preciadas, la una
> para el cavallero que vinciesse los torneos y la otra para el que
> mejor justasse, y puso esta copa para los baxos que en aquella
> tierra se precian mucho de luchar y ante los novios hobo
> muchos que lucharon y como yo allí me fallé y vi esta copa
> tan rica esforcéme a luchar y fue mi ventura que la gané.
> (Chs. 98 and 99, fol. 112 [xcii])

Don Duardos' explanation reminds Flérida of the low social status
he pretends to have while at the same time it insists on his accomp-
lishment in winning the cup. His use of the word *luchar* underscores the erotic activity which figures so largely in the romance; an
English-speaking reader may be reminded of the wrestling match
which first draws Rosalind's attention to Orlando. In Vicente's play
the word *luchas* is used in a much more general sense. We should
probably translate it here simply as "struggles".

Vicente often proceeds in the opposite way, adding material that
is not present, or is only implied, in *Primaleón*. A good example is
the scene in which Flérida's ladies-in-waiting first meet Don Duardos
(675-95). Vicente's point of departure is the following passage:

Y como las donzellas lo vieron ansí estar mudo començaron
de reír de él y dixeron:

—Entiendo que en balde fue éste tan fermoso, que deve de
ser tan sandío que no sabe qué dezir.

Artada, que cabe la infanta estava, les dixo:

—Yo creo que él es mudo. Preguntémosgelo si lo es o por
qué calla ansí.

— Bien será—dixeron las donzellas.

Y Artada le dixo:

—Ay, amigo, ¿vos tenéis atada la lengua o por qué no
fabláis a la infanta? (Ch. 98, fol. 91)

Vicente adds a comic note by having these gentle ladies of the court
make fun of Don Duardos and threaten to duck him in a pond. At
the same time he arouses our sympathy for Don Duardos by sub-
jecting him to verbal abuse.

The attempt by Julián and his wife to persuade Don Duardos to
marry the peasant girl Grimanesa (1374-83) has no counterpart in
Primaleón. The edition of the *Copilaçam* published in Lisbon in
1586 introduces Grimanesa herself. The passage begins immediately
after line 1402 of the Clásicos Castellanos text:

Julián.   los dedos tuertos y gruessos,
                     crespa la ceja y babosa,
                     pretellona y graciosa,
                     ¡juro a tal que hasta los huessos
                     es bueno para la cosa
                     Grimanesa!

Grimanesa.	Hola.
Julián.	Ven acá.
Grimanesa.	Heisme aquí. ¿Que me queréis?
Julián.	He aquí la moça do está.
	Esta creo que será
	buena para . . . ya sabéis.
Costanza.	¿Queréis casar, hija mía,
	con este nuestro criado?
Grimanesa.	Con éste sí casaría.
Don Duardos.	¡Cómo tardas, alegría!
	¡Quán presto vienes, cuidado!
Grimanesa.	¡Y un hombre tan hermoso!
	Pues tirado este sayal
	es él para ser esposo
	de Artada. Estáis donoso:
	no casa assí hombre tal.
Julián.	Mirad. Vos sois estrangero,
	la moça no descuidada,
	bien quista y aparentada.
	Tiene un asno y un sendero;
	trataréis en membrillada.
Costanza.	Si bien quisieres casar,
	estímate, Grimanesa.
	¿Quién te manda a ti abaxar?
Grimanesa.	Mas ¿qué aprovecha alterar
	para tal cosa como essa?
Don Duardos.	El que casa ha de casar
	con tan sobrado plazer
	como yo tengo pesar.
	No hago sino cavar;
	escóndeseme el haver.
	No tengo de tomar muger
	hasta que el tesoro mío
	no lo tenga en mi poder;
	entonces el mi querer
	mostrará gran poderío.
	Andad por Dios en buen hora.
	Íos. Dexadme cavar.

No desprecio esta señora,
mas no puedo por agora
ni casar ni descansar.[8]

Reckert believes that the scene was omitted from the *Copilaçam* of 1562 because Vicente's son Luís found it inappropriate to the "dulce retórica y escogido estilo" of the rest of the play. He believes, too, that, like the appearance of Camilote and Maimonda earlier in the play, it is "uno de los contrapuntos estéticos sabiamente introducidos en esta y otras piezas de Gil Vicente para aliviar la tensión afectiva" (*8*, 391). The comic force of the scene is undeniable. Grimanesa appears immediately after her name has been mentioned by Julián, just as Aires Rosado makes his first appearance in *Quem tem farelos?* reading aloud from his *cancioneiro* immediately after his servant has mentioned the book.[9] I do not believe, however, that we should see the introduction of Grimanesa as lessening the emotional tension of the play. On the contrary: the scene serves to heighten our sympathy for Don Duardos by showing the humiliation to which he has willingly subjected himself by pretending to be the gardener's son. The scene is a perfect counterpart of the one earlier in the play when Flérida's ladies-in-waiting make fun of Don Duardos because he hesitates to speak with them (675-95).

Sometimes Vicente makes "scene" of material which in *Primaleón* is presented as "summary".[10] In doing so he often adds a comic touch of his own. When Don Duardos first seeks admission to the *huerta* the gardener's children argue about which of them will go to see who is knocking at the gate (528-41). An exchange of compliments between Julián and his wife follows; the knocking at the gate has apparently been quite forgotten. Though the gardener's wife and children are indeed mentioned at this point in *Primaleón* (Ch. 97, fols 90, 90^v), the scene is Vicente's invention. Here, as often in his plays, several things are going on at once. The dialogue between Julián and his sons is not only funny in itself but contrasts

---

8   The scene is printed in Anselmo Braamcamp Freire, *Vida e obras de Gil Vicente* (Lisbon: Ocidente, 1944), pp. 433-4, and in *8*, 391-5.

9   See my edition in *Farces* (see Ch. 3, note 1), lines 149-52, and the comments by Maria Teresa Rita cited in the Introduction, pp. 29-30.

10 I borrow these useful terms from Phyllis Bentley, *Some Observations on the Art of Narrative* (New York: Macmillan, 1948).

sharply with the exchange of compliments with his wife which follows. The latter exchange, in turn, foreshadows later developments in its marvellous evocation of the *huerta*, which, as we have observed in the chapter on "Imagery", symbolizes Flérida herself. The dialogue between Julián and his wife further underscores the theme of the irresistible force of love on which the whole play is centered.[11] Finally, the scene serves to increase the audience's suspense as it waits to learn who is knocking at the gate. It contrasts Don Duardos' impatience to be admitted to the *huerta* — which might easily be conveyed by making each series of knocks on the gate louder than the one before — with the indifference of Juan and his family toward learning the identity of their visitor.

Another, more fully developed, example of the way Vicente adds to his source is his treatment of Camilote and Maimonda. Both appear in *Primaleón*, where Camilote is described as a *salvaje* (fol. 115 [xcv]). He is not, however, the traditional wild man who represents lust and is presented as the antithesis of the courtly lover.[12] In *Primaleón*, as in Vicente's play, Camilote is every inch the courtly lover, just as much so as Don Duardos himself. He certainly does not symbolize what Parker calls "the bestial side of human nature". Rather, his role is to remind us that no one can resist the power of love, a point made explicitly by the Emperor in *Don Duardos* (272-82) in answer to Flérida's naïve question:

¿Quién hizo cosas tan feas,
namoradas? (270-1)

This kind of wild man is a newer creation than the lustful beast studied by Parker but he, too, has a well established place in literary history: Camilote is a direct descendant of the wild man who appears in several fifteenth-century Spanish sentimental novels. Vicente makes such a wild man one of the principal characters of his *Comédia sobra a divisa da cidade de Coimbra*.[13]

---

[11] See *10*, 762-3.

[12] See A.A. Parker, "Expansion and Scholarship in Spain", in Denys Hay, ed., *The Age of the Renaissance* (London: Thames and Hudson, 1967), p. 241.

[13] See Alan D. Deyermond, "El hombre salvaje en la novela sentimental", *Filología*, X (1964), 97-111.

Vicente, however, turns away from *Primaleón* by treating Camilote as a comic figure. The dialogue between him and Maimonda (109-24, 313-18) is Vicente's addition. In *Primaleón* Maimonda does not speak at this point and Camilote's words are reasonable enough, given the conventions of the romances of chivalry. They are ridiculous only because of the grotesqueness of Camilote and Maimonda. In *Don Duardos*, Camilote is blind not only to Maimonda's ugliness but to its moral counterpart, her absurd conceit.[14] Vicente treats the whole scene primarily as a comic interlude, but he uses it also to underscore some central themes of the play.

William Empson's discussion of double plots in the second chapter of his book *Some Versions of Pastoral* has interesting implications for *Don Duardos*, as it has also for the Spanish *comedia* of the seventeenth century. Empson observes that the comic interlude may serve as a simple form of double plot: "The comic part relieves boredom and the strain of belief in the serious part, but this need not imply criticism of it."[15] On the contrary: "The play can thus anticipate the parody a hearer might have in mind without losing its dignity, which thus has a sort of completeness" (28). It is perhaps because he wished to anticipate, and thus to forestall, the audience's temptation to see Don Duardos' love as absurdly exaggerated that Vicente moves Camilote's arrival at the Emperor's court closer to the beginning of the play. (In *Primaleón* it comes after, not before, Flérida has met Don Duardos in his disguise as the gardener's son.) He may also have felt that the scene would clash with the tone of "suave melancolía"—the phrase is Dámaso Alonso's— which becomes increasingly intense as Don Duardos begins to doubt whether Flérida will ever return his love for her and as she struggles to maintain the aloofness appropriate toward one who is not her equal in rank.

Don Duardos holds a special place in Vicente's theater. It is the finest of his Spanish plays and perhaps even of all that he wrote. The very fact that Vicente follows his source, *Primaleón*, so closely makes it the one of his plays in which we can best perceive his

14 See *15*, 5.

15 *Some Versions of Pastoral* (1935; rpt. Norfolk, Conn.: New Directions, 1960), p. 26.

originality. An examination of the ways in which Vicente adapts these borrowed materials to his own purposes can teach us a great deal about the way his mind worked. It may take us as close as we can get to observing the creative process at work in him.

Bibliographical Note

BIBLIOGRAPHY

The most recent and reliable is C.C. Stathatos, *A Gil Vicente Bibliography (1940-1975)*, Research Bibliographies and Checklists, 30 (London: Grant and Cutler, 1980).

BACKGROUND

The best account in English, particularly good on social history, is A.H. de Oliveira Marques, *History of Portugal.* I. *From Lusitania to Empire* (New York: Columbia Univ. Press, 1972). An extremely readable treatment of many topics of interest to students of Vicente's theater is C.R. Boxer, *The Portuguese Seaborne Empire 1415-1825* (London: Hutchinson, 1969). There is no recent history of Portuguese literature in English, though Aubrey F.G. Bell's *Portuguese Literature* (Oxford: Clarendon Press, 1922) still retains much of its value. Good treatments in Portuguese include Hernâni Cidade, *Lições de cultura e literatura portuguesas* (5th ed., Coimbra: Coimbra Editora, 1968), and António José Saraiva and Óscar Lopes, *História da literatura portuguesa* (4th ed., Oporto: Porto Editora, [1964]). The fullest account of the development of the theater in Portugal is Luciana Stegagno Picchio, *História do teatro português*, trans. Manuel de Lucena (Lisbon: Portugália, 1969).

EDITIONS

The indispensable starting point for all modern editions of Vicente's plays is *Obras completas de Gil Vicente. Reimpressão "fac-similada" da edição de 1562* (Lisbon: Oficinas Gráficas da Biblioteca Nacional, 1928). This facsimile edition is not, however, completely trustworthy; see *8*, below, pp. 197-223. Both text and notes in Marques Braga's edition of Vicente's *Obras completas*, 6 vols (Lisbon: Sá da Costa, 1942-44), are unreliable. For *Don Duardos* alone there is:

1. Dámaso Alonso, ed., *Tragicomedia de Don Duardos*, I (Madrid:

Consejo Superior de Investigaciones Científicas, 1942). A superb annotated edition of the text as given in the *Copilaçam* of 1562 and two masterful essays, "La poesía dramática en la *Tragicomedia de Don Duardos*" and "Problemas del castellano vicentino". "La poesía dramática" is reprinted in his *Ensayos sobre poesía española* (Buenos Aires: Revista de Occidente Argentina, 1946), pp. 125-44.

CRITICAL STUDIES

2. Margit Frenk Alatorre, *Estudios sobre lírica antigua* (Madrid: Castalia, 1978). A useful collection of sixteen previously published articles, some of which are of fundamental importance for the understanding of Vicente's lyrics.

3. Eugenio Asensio, *Poética y realidad en el cancionero peninsular de la Edad Media* (2nd ed., Madrid: Gredos, 1970). The splendid essay "Gil Vicente y las cantigas paralelísticas 'restauradas' " (pp. 134-76) ranges much more widely than its title implies and offers a number of insights into Vicente's theater.

4. Giuseppina Ledda,"Note sul *Primaleón* o *Libro segundo del emperador Palmerín*", in *Studi sul 'Palmerín de Olivia'.* III. *Saggi e ricerche* (Pisa, 1966), pp. 137-58. A sympathetic reading of the romance of chivalry which was the principal source of *Don Duardos*.

5. María Rosa Lida de Malkiel, "Para la génesis del *Auto de la sibila Casandra*", *Filología*, V (1959), 47-63; rpt. in her *Estudios de literatura española y comparada* (Buenos Aires: Eudeba [Editorial Universitaria de Buenos Aires], 1966), pp. 157-72. In a note at the end of the essay the author observes that her work was completed before the appearance of the studies by Spitzer (*12*) and Révah (*9*), which to some extent supersede it.

6. Melveena McKendrick, *Woman and Society in the Spanish Drama of the Golden Age: A Study of the 'Mujer varonil'* (Cambridge: Univ. Press, 1974). McKendrick's feminist reading of *Casandra* (pp. 45-51) is interesting, though she perhaps gives too little attention to the play's theological content.

7. A.A. Parker, *The Approach to the Spanish Drama of the Golden Age*, Diamante, VI (London: The Hispanic and Luso-Brazilian Councils, 1957). Basic to an understanding of the similarities and differences between Vicente's theater and the later *comedia*.

8. Stephen Reckert, *Gil Vicente: espíritu y letra*. I. *Estudios* (Madrid: Gredos, 1977). The most comprehensive book on Vicente in many years. Reckert's analysis of the two versions of *Don Duardos* (pp. 236-469) will be indispensable to future students of the play.

9. I.S. Révah, "L'*Auto de la Sibylle Cassandre* de Gil Vicente", *Hispanic Review*, XXVII (1959), 167-93. The most authoritative account of the play's sources.

10. Elias L. Rivers, "The Unity of *Don Duardos*", *Modern Language Notes*, LXXVI (1961), 759-66. Argues persuasively that everything in the play, including the episode of Camilote and Maimonda, may be seen as a variation on the basic theme of love.

11. N.D. Shergold, *A History of the Spanish Stage from Medieval Times until the End of the Seventeenth Century* (Oxford: Clarendon Press, 1967). The standard account of the staging of plays in the Peninsula. The final chapter offers some stimulating pages on the ways in which a knowledge of stage conditions can contribute to literary appreciation of the plays.

12. Leo Spitzer, "The Artistic Unity of Gil Vicente's *Auto da sibila Cassandra*", *Hispanic Review*, XXVII (1959), 56-77. Probably the best single essay on the play.

13. John Stevens, *Music and Poetry in the Early Tudor Court* (London: Methuen, 1961). A marvellously evocative account of courtly society in England which throws much light on sixteenth-century Hispanic literature.

14. Paul Teyssier, *La Langue de Gil Vicente* (Paris: C. Klincksieck, 1959). The classic treatment of Vicente's use of both Spanish and Portuguese.

15. Bruce W. Wardropper, "Approaching the Metaphysical Sense of Gil Vicente's Chivalric Tragicomedies", *Bulletin of the*

Comediantes, XVI (1964), 1-9. An application to *Don Duardos* and *Amadís de Gaula* of the analysis of imagery which Wardropper has used in a number of important studies of the *comedia*. See also his essay "The Implicit Craft of the Spanish *comedia*", in *Studies in Spanish Literature of the Golden Age Presented to Edward M. Wilson*, ed. R.O. Jones (London: Tamesis, 1973), pp. 339-56.

[fol. 91] Capítulo xcviii. Cómo la hortelana llevó a don Duardos delante la infanta Flérida y cómo le dixo que era un su hijo que havía días que se havía ido de aquella tierra y cómo la infanta hovo plazer con su vista.

Venida la tarde la infanta Flérida con la fermosa Amandria, fija del rey de Esperte, que con ella havía quedado por amor de Abenucque que el emperador rogó a su padre que ge la diesse por muger y él ge la otorgó mas no los havían desposado porque era muy niña y ella dezía que fasta que Flérida se casasse que ella no se havía de desposar. E ansimesmo se criava con la infanta una fija del duque Tolome y de Brionela su muger y esta donzella se llamava Artada y era muy fermosa y sesuda. La infanta Flérida la amava más que a ninguna de sus donzellas por su gran bondad. Y la infanta Flérida con sus donzellas ansí como solían se fueron a la huerta y Flérida se sentó cabe las fuentes, que allí folgava ella mucho, y la hortelana vino a ella muy leda y diole de las rosas y flores en la mano y díxole:

—Mi señora, ¿no vedes vos la mi alegría? Sabed que hoy he fallado un fijo que ha mucho tiempo que se me fue y él viene tan grande y fermoso que a duro lo puedo conoscer.

—De todo vuestro plazer—dixo Flérida*—lo recibo yo y mucho me plaze porque escusará a Julián vuestro marido de afán.

—Esso podéis vos, mi señora, dezir von verdad—dixo la hortelana —que él es tal que es toda nuestra alegría.

Y esto dezía ella por el tesoro que de él esperava.

—Amiga—dixo la infanta—, traédmelo que lo quiero ver.

La hortelana fue dando bozes. —Fijo Julián—dezía ella—, venid, que mi señora Flérida vos quiere ver.

Quando don Duardos lo oyó el coraçón se le enflaqueció porque ya él la havía visto entre los árboles. Con la gran vergüença de parescer delante de ella tal y con el grande amor que le havía no podía mover los pies para ir adelante. La hortelana lo llevó por la mano y lo llevó ante Flérida.

---

* Flérida] flarida

—Ay, señora—dixo ella—, ¿no tengo yo razón de ser la mi alegría grande por cobrar tal fijo?

—Sí, por cierto—dixo la infanta—, y dígovos que mal parece a su padre. Él venga en buena hora.

Julián estava ante su señora tan ledo que no podía fablar y quando F[l]érida le dixo que viniesse en buena hora homillóse ante ella que fablalle no pudo y estovo ansí gran pieça que jamás los ojos partió de ella y el coraçón suyo era folgado de ver a su señora y dezía entre sí que mucha razón tenía de amalla ansí tan afincadamente. Y como las donzellas lo vieron ansí estar mudo començaron de reír de él y dixeron:

—Entiendo que en balde fue éste tan fermoso, que deve de ser tan sandío que no sabe qué dezir.

Artada, que cabe la infanta estava, les dixo:

—Yo creo que él es mudo. Preguntémosgelo si lo es o por qué calla ansí.

—Bien será—dixeron las donzellas.

Y Artada le dixo:

—Ay, amigo, ¿vos tenéis atada la lengua o por qué no fabláis a la infanta?

—Ay, señora—dixo Julián—, el coraçón que está espantado de la maravilla que los ojos veen tiene presa la lengua que no fable.

—¿Y qué maravilla es essa?—dixo Artada.

—¿Qué maravilla puedo mayor ver—dixo Julián—que ver la gran fermosura de vosotras? Cierto, yo he visto muchas dueñas y donzellas en otras tierras adonde he anda(n)do y nunca vi ninguna que a la menor de vosotras se igualasse y por esto estava yo callando, pensando quánta bienaventurança he alcança(n)do en venir a este lugar para vos poder servir, y si yo no fuere tal que lo merezca fazer, vosotras sois de tanta bondad que miraréis a la voluntad con que yo lo fiziere. Y dígovos que no me da ninguna cosa del escarnio que de mí fezistes, que bien veo que lo merezco, que no deviera de ser osado de parecer ante vosotras, mas fízelo yo por fazer el mandado de mi madre. Y de aquí adelante yo vos entiendo de servir tanto que enmiende el yerro que fize.

—Amigo—dixo Artada—, esse yerro y más que vos fagáis vos será perdonado, que bien vemos que vuestra persona es tal que podrá servir bien en los servicios que fasta aquí vuestro padre ha servido.

—Esso faré yo— dixo Julián.

Y la infanta Flérida rio muy fermoso de las razones que Artada con Julián havía passado y díxole:

—Ay, amiga, déxate de estar en razones con Julián, que yo te digo que él es más sesudo según me parece que vosotras mesuradas que de él es[fol. 91ᵛ]carnio fazéis.

Y tornóse para Julián y díxole:

—Amigo, dexad estas sandías y no paréis mientes a sus dichos, que con el poco seso que tienen hablan cosas desconcertadas y de aquí adelante servid lealmente como faze vuestro padre que yo vos digo que yo vos precio mucho por amor de ellos y dígovos que vuestra apostura que en otro oficio mejor vos quisiera yo ver que en éste, mas ¡ay! havrá tiempo para fazeros mercedes, que por amor de vuestros padres es razón que yo vos las faga.

Julián fue muy ledo con aquella razón y fue a fincar los hinojos ante la infanta y por fuerça le tomó la mano y ge la besó y díxole:

—Mi señora, bien creo yo que según el vuestro gran valor y bondad faréis grandes los mis pequeños servicios y me daréis mayor galardón que yo por ellos merezca.

La infanta, que vido las muy fermosas manos de Julián, maravillóse en su coraçón y dixo:

—Por cierto, estas manos no son de villano ni ansimesmo las razones.

Y aunque esto pensó no lo dio a entender y levantóse y andovo por la huerta a su sabor y don Dúardos quedó muy ledo por le haver besado las manos y por lo que le dixo y poníase en los lugares adonde la podía ver más a su voluntad. Mas sabed que aunque las donzellas fizieron escarnio de él, muy maravilladas eran de ver la su fermosura que sabed que don Duardos estrañamente era apuesto y de allí adelante poníanlo en muchas razones y él le respondía tan bien que ellas eran maravilladas.

Y desque fue tiempo la infanta se fue a su cámara y Julián quedó ansí como aquél que queda ascuras quitándole la claridad delante de sí y si la primera vez que la vido le pareció fermosa muy más le pareció entonces y si fasta allí él cuitas padecía de allí adelante las sintió y dezía en su coraçón:

—¡Ay, don Duardos, quánto bien te faría Dios si tú pudiesses

acabar lo que has començado! Tú alcançarías la mayor gloria que
nunca cavallero alcançó y que haviendo a Flérida en tu poder que
descansaría tu coraçón y vengaría la injuria de tu avuelo.

Y con esto tornó muy ledo en su coraçón y teníase por bien
andante de haver cobrado aquel lugar. Y él se supo haver tan sesuda-
mente con los hortelanos que mucho lo amavan y acordó de traer
la copa y fazer entender a los hortelanos que la havía havido del
tesoro y que la diessen a Flérida porque huviesse alguna parte de
aquello que le pertenecía y salió a hablar con su escudero y tomóle
todo el haver que traía y la copa y mandóle que fuesse a la infanta
por más de lo que le tenía en guarda y que le dixesse de la manera
que quedava y que le embiasse unas armas y un cavallo a la villa
adonde Belagriz estava. Y sabed que en aquel tiempo el emperador
tenía pazes con los moros y todos passavan de una parte a otra
seguramente y el emperador supo de lo que el Cavallero del Can
fizo por fazer cobrar a Mosderín su señorío y mucho lo preciava
en su voluntad aunque le tenía enemistad por haver perdido por
él a Primaleón, que de otra manera él preciara mucho por la su gran
bondad. El escudero se fue con aquel mandado a la infanta Olimba y
de camino vido al infante Belagriz que muy ledo fue por saber del
Cavallero del Can. El escudero le dixo cómo quedava.

—Ay Dios—dixo Belagriz—, y qué poder tan grande es el del
amor que un cavallero que par no tiene ansí sean atadas sus fuerças
por una donzella que lo faga venir en tanta baxeza. Yo lo querría
ver si cava tan bien la tierra como tiene poder y fuerça en las armas
mas según él es entendido a todo se sabrá dar maña.

Y luego el escudero se partió de allí y la infanta Olimba hovo
mucho plazer con él y le preguntó que qué tal quedava el Cavallero
del Can. El escudero ge lo contó todo como havéis oído. A la infanta
le vinieron las lágrimas a los ojos de compassión y luego ella lo tornó
a embiar con mucho haver y fizo fazer unas armas blancas muy
fuertes y ricas y eran tales que a duro se podrían fallar mejores y
hovo un cavallo blanco muy estremado de bueno y embiólo todo a
Belagriz para que lo tuviesse guardado si el Cavallero del Can lo
embiasse a pedir y embiógelo con Clodio, el donzel de don Duardos,
que no se podía sofrir de estar tan lexos de su señor y llevó consigo
a Mayortes, el gran can, que no se quiso apartar de él, y allí tenían
ellos sabrosa vida con Belagriz andando a caça, mas más sabrosa vida

tenía don Duardos llamándose Julián, el qual desque embió el
escudero a la infanta Olimba se tornó para la huerta y escondió
muy bien la copa y el haver fasta otro día de mañana [fol.
92*] que fizo (en) entender a Julián el hortola(na)no que lo havía sacado
del tesoro que allí era. No hay hombre que vos pudiesse dezir la
alegría de ambos a dos viéndose de pobres ricos. Y don Duardos
les dixo:

—Amigos, de la parte que a mí me cabe de este tesoro quiero yo
dar a la infanta Flérida esta copa por que beva porque es razón que
haya alguna parte pues le viene de derecho y hoy si aquí viniere a
la huerta sacalda y dalde a bever con ella que yo le diré tal razón
de dónde la huve que ella no entienda en nuestra fazienda.

—Fijo Julián—dixo la hortelana—, todo quanto vos quisierdes
faré yo de gana. Mirad vos que no nos perdamos por dárgela.

—No perderéis—dixo Julián—, que ante vos digo que nos ganare-
mos.

—Ansí quiera Dios—dixeron ellos.

Y aquel día salió la infanta Flérida a la huerta como solía y
sentóse cabe las fuentes y don Duardos le traxo de la fruta que
comiesse.

—Julián amigo, ¿cómo te va en esta tierra?

—Vame, señora, mejor que jamás me fue, pues soy aquí para
serviros.

—Tu fazes bien—dixo la infanta—en estar aquí, que mejor te
irá que andando por tierras estrañas.

—Esso es gran verdad—dixo Julián.

Y estando ellos fablando en esto vino la hortelana con la copa
y díxole:

—Mi señora Flérida, pues havéis comido de la fruta razón es que
beváis dell agua con esta copa tan fermosa.

—Ay, amiga—dixo la infanta—, ¿y de dónde huvistes tan rica copa
como ésta?

—Sabed, señora—dixo ella—, que mi fijo Julián me la traxo y yo
quiérovosla dar que para vos y no para mí es tan preciada cosa.

—Ruégote, amigo Julián—dixo la infanta—, que me digas quién
te la dio.

—Yo vos lo diré, mi señora—dixo Julián—, pues vos me lo mandáis.
[fol. 94ᵛ] Capítulo ci. Cómo, estando el emperador Palmerín en su
palacio con muchos altos hombres, entró por las puertas un hombre
muy feo con una donzella muy desemejada por la [fol. 95*] mano y
suplicó al emperador que le dies[s]e orden de cavallería y de lo que
le avino después que la rescibió.

Luego otro día la emperatriz, estando Flérida para se ir a la
huerta, embió por ella para ir a ver al emperador que havía días que
no lo havía visto. Que sabed que el emperador jamás entrava en la
cámara de Flérida ni en la huerta donde solían estar. Y por esto
estava él bien seguro que no lo viesse y el emperador folgó mucho
de ver a Flérida y pescudóle qué tal estava la su huerta. Ella dixo
que [e]stava mejor que jamás estuvo. Y sabed que con el emperador
estavan muchos altos hombres que venían por lo ver por amor de
la ida de Primaleón y todos eran muy tristes porque no sabían
nuevas de él.

Y estando todos, como vos dezimos, en el gran palacio, entró
en él el escudero, que traía por la mano una donzella y ambos
a dos eran tan feos que no havía hombre que los viesse que de
ellos no se espantasse. Él era alto de cuerpo y membrudo, era todo
velloso que parescía salvaje, y de aquella manera venía vestido
que traía los braços de fuera que parescían bien sus cabellos y
la ropa era muy corta y abrochávase delante con una broncha
de oro. Y la donzella venía vestida de una seda de muchas colores
y traíala cercada de piedras muy buenas y encima de su cabeça
no traía cosa y ella tenía los cabellos muy negros y cortos y crespos
a maravilla y traía la garganta muy seca y negra de fuera. Y venían
ambos a dos tan desemejados que a todos pusieron espanto y venían
bien acompañados. Ambos a dos fueron fincar las rodillas ante el
emperador y todos callavan por oír y ver qué demanda traían
y el escudero feo desque besó las manos al emperador díxole:

—Mi señor, yo soy vuestro natural y vengo a vos pedir por merced
que me fagáis cavallero porque yo prometí a esta donzella de no lo
ser sino de mano del más alto hombre y mejor que huvies[s]e en
el mundo y bien sé que en todo él no hay quien con vos se iguale

* fol. 95] fo. cxv

y por esto quiero yo ser cavallero de vuestra mano por que de vos me
venga ardimiento.

El emperador que tan bien lo oyó razonar díxole:

—Amigo, a mí me plaze de vos fazer cavallero mas mucho quería
saber quién sois y cómo vos llaman porque vea si merescéis de ser
cavallero.

—No dudéis, señor, de me fazer cavallero que yo vos digo que yo
soy fidalgo y vengo de linaje de cavalleros en quien siempre hovo
bondad y ardimiento. Y pues queréis saber mi fazienda quiérovosla
dezir. Sabed, señor, que nosotros somos de tierra de Gorate y esta
donzella es fija del señor de ella y él no hovo sino otra fija que
heredó la tierra por ser mayor. Y esta donzella, desque vido a su
hermana señora de la tierra, apartóse a un castillo y allí fazía vida
saliendo muchas vezes al campo a caçar. Y yo soy fijo de un cavallero
que hay en aquella tierra y tiene un castillo en lo más cercano a las
grandes montañas que en aquella tierra hay. Ansimesmo desde
pequeño usé las caças y un día acaesció me amatar un puerco ante
este señora que cabe una fuente estava apeada por folgar. Y como
ella me vido tan valiente y ligero preció me mucho y desde aquella
hora que yo la vi y ella vido a mí començámonos de amar muy
afincadamente y yo le pedí por merced que se doliesse de mí y ella
me otorgó su amor. Y quando yo hove alcançado tanto bien cres-
cióme el argullo y juréle me fazer cavallero por mano de[l] mejor
cavallero que viviesse en el mundo y de allí adelante de fazer tales
cosas en armas que todo el mundo dixe[s]se que jamás donzella
tuvo tal amigo y de ganalle tierra y señorío por donde passasse a su
hermana en valor. Maimonda, que ansí se llama esta donzella, fue
muy leda con la promessa que yo le fize y díxome que ella quería
venir comigo a ver mis grandes fechos y yo ge lo tuve en merced y
tráxela comigo y dígovos que jamás hombre alcançó tan gran don
como yo en havella alcançado por señora.

El emperador no pude estar que no riesse y ansimesmo todos los
altos hombres que con él estavan y dezían:

—Cierto, la fermosura de la donzella es tanta que sus fuerças farán
ser el cavallero de grande ardimiento. Viéndola ante sí no deve turar
cavallero en silla mucho tiempo.

Y dezían otras cosas de escarnio. La infanta Flérida, acordándo-
sele de la fermosura de su Julián, fízose muy loçana y començó de

reír con sus donzellas de*l** escudero y de la donzella.

Camilote, que ansí se llamava el escudero feo, bien vido la burla que la infanta y los cavalleros le fazían y por entonces sufrióse que no dixo nada. El emperador dixo:

—Amigo, pues que tan fermosa amiga [fol. 95^v] tenéis, razón es de fazer vos su ruego por que veamos lo que por ella faréis.

Y luego Camilote fizo traer sus armas, que eran muy fuertes más que ricas, y armóse de ellas y quatro escuderos que traía lo armaron muy aína y desque fue todo armado el emperador lo fizo cavallero y como Camilote se vido fecho cavallero fue muy ledo y dixo:

—Agora, cavalleros del emperador, es hora de fazer escarnio de mí y de mi donzella, que no fasta aquí.

Y como esto dixo fuese para un escudero de los suyos y sacóle de baxo del manto una guirlanda de rosas, las más fermosas y de estraña color que jamás allí vieron, y como él las sacó de baxo del manto todo el palacio fue lleno de olor maravilloso. Camilote fue a poner la guirlanda de las rosas a Maimonda su donzella encima de la su cabeça y dixo:

—Yo quiero ver quál cavallero será tan osado que de aquí vos quite esta guirlanda. Y sabed, señor emperador, que estas rosas hove yo con mucho afán y peligro y entiéndolas agora de defender mejor, que soy cavallero y demándovos licencia para estar en el campo que tenéis fecho para los cavalleros que uno por otro se combaten tanto quanto fuere mi voluntad. Y yo quiero tener comigo mi donzella y veamos quién será tan fardido que la guirlanda de la cabeça le vaya a tomar.

El emperador estovo dudando de le otorgar su demanda porque conosció que devía ser de grandes fuerças y el duque de Amenón, que allí estava, que era cavallero mancebo y muy ardid y afincadamente amava a Liserma, fija del duque de Pera, que era estremada en fermosura y entendíase él de casar con ella, dixo al emperador quando le vido tardar en la respuesta:

—Señor, ¿qué fazéis que no otorgáis a Camilote lo que vos demanda? Gran deshonra sería de todos vuestros cavalleros si Maimonda llevasse assí la guirlanda tan ligeramente. Pídovos por merced que se lo otorguéis y le deis seguro.

*de*l] des

Todos los otros cavalleros dezían que el duque dezía gran verdad. El emperador, que vido su voluntad, dixo a Camilote:

—Amigo, a la hora que vos quisierdes podréis entrar en el campo y esperar allí los que contra vos quisieren ir y yo vos aseguro que por mal ni bien que vos avenga no rescibáis daño salvo de aquellos que con vos *se** quisieren combatir. Y ruégovos que me digáis dónde huvistes rosas tan olorosas para essa guirlanda.

Camilote fue muy ledo quando el emperador le otorgó el seguro.

—A Dios plega, señor—dixo él—, que yo vos pueda servir la merced que me fezistes. Y sabed que estas rosas hay en mi tierra en un árbol muy preciado, el qual está en la más alta montaña que hay en tierra del Gorate y fasta hoy ninguno pudo coger de él rosas aunque son de gran virtud y tura siete años que no se secan mas todavía están ansí como las veis y yo solo *he*** s(e)ido el que las he cogido por el mi grande esfuerço. Sabed que en la montaña hay muchas bestias fieras de estrañas maneras por donde los hombres de la tierra no son osados de entrar en ella salvo yo. Desque Maimonda mi señora me otorgó su amor me cresció tanto el esfuerço que osé sobir en la montaña y maté a[s]saz de bestias fieras en ella y traxe las rosas a pesar de todas y fize esta guirlanda de ellas para venir aquí.

El emperador hovo gran plazer de ver a Camilote tan enamorado de aquella donzella tan desemejada y bolvióse con alegre cara contra la emperatriz Polinarda y díxole:

—¿Cre[é]is vos, señora, que si vos fuérades tan fermosa como aquella donzella que no me di[é]rades mayores fuerzas para començar acabar mayores fechos de los que fize por vuestro servicio?

La emperatriz se le acordó de aquel sabroso tiempo y tornó muy loçana y dixo al emperador:

—Creo yo, mi señor, que de ella a mí hay poca ventaja y si vos grandes fechos fezistes acabásteslos por el vuestro grande ardimiento.

—Esso no consiento yo que digáis, señora—dixo el emperador—, que agora mejor que nunca me osaría yo combatir sobre essa razón con Camilote y con otro cavallero mejor y le faría conocer que en todo el mundo otra más fermosa que vos [no] hovo ni havrá.

Y quando esto dixo encendióse el rostro mucho con grande

  * *se*] le
 ** *he*] &

ardimiento como si delante de sí tuviera quien le contradixera su razón. Todos folgaron de oíllos y más Flérida que entonces començava amar. Fue muy leda de oír el estraño amor que su padre y madre tuvieron y pensava ella que no menos sería el suyo con Julián si él cavallero fuesse que la meresciesse y desacordadamente dixo:

—Cierto, señor(a), con mayor razón fezistes vos tan grandes fechos que Camilote los fará por aquella donzella que tan [fol. 96] desemejada es. Más le valiera estar allá en su tierra con las bestias, salvajes como ellos son, que no venir acá a espantarnos que en balde es el afán del novel cavallero.

El emperador y todos riyeron de lo que Flérida dixo salvo Camilote que fue contra ella muy airado y fue tanta su saña que de los ojos parecía que le salían centellas de fuego y ansimesmo de su rostro y con boz muy temerosa le dixo:

—En mal punto, donzella, fuestes tan fermosa para ser tan desmesurada. Dígovos que Maimonda es tan amada de mí como vos lo seréis por más fermosa que seáis y ver quiero yo si por vuestra fermosura havrá cavallero tan ardid que comigo se ose combatir y gane la guirlanda para que vos pongáis encima de vuestros fermosos cabellos. ¿Qué? ¿Cuidáis vos que mejor os parecería que a esta mi señora? Pues ya no me ayude Dios si vos seáis tan bien andante aunque seáis tan fermosa que en vuestras manos la toméis. Maimonda la hovo por grande amor que yo le tengo y con esto ge la entiendo de defender y vengan contra mí quantos cavalleros quisieren.

La infanta fue muy espantada a maravilla quando vido a Camilote tan airado contra ella y bolvióse contra el emperador perdida la color de temor. El emperador se rio y dixo a Camilote:

—Amigo, idvos en buena hora al campo adonde havéis de estar y mostra vuestra saña contra los cavalleros y no contra las donzellas que si ansí espantáis a ellos como fazéis a las donzellas a duro vos podrá durar ninguno en campo.

—Ansí lo faré—dixo Camilote.

Y luego tomó a Maimonda por la mano y fuese con ella y el emperador mandó a un cavallero que fuesse con él y lo metiesse en el campo y que con dozientos cavalleros tuviesse la guarda mientra el allí estuviesse por que ninguno le fiziesse mal sino aquellos que con él se quisiessen ir a combatir y el cavallero lo fizo y Camilote se fue al campo con su compaña y allí fizo fincar una tienda para Maimonda.

Ora sabed que todo lo que Camilote dixo al emperador de su fazienda era verdad y en aquella tierra de Gorate eran todas las gentes
como salvajes y eran muy bravos y esquivos contra otras gentes y
havía en ella grandes montañas y esta tierra es en el fin de Grecia
fazia el mediodía y Maimonda era fija del señor de aquella tierra y
Camilote de otro cavallero que era so vassallo y por esso era él tan
preciado en ser de ella amado y él salió de tan gran fuerça y coraçón
que no havía bestia fiera que contra él se comparasse que con una
maça que en las manos traía matava quantas fallava y quando él
subió a la alta montaña por las rosas mató muchos leones y tigres
y otras bestias de estrañas maneras y con esto era él tan argulloso y
jamás ninguno de aquella tierra fue osado de fazer lo que él fizo
aunque sabían de algunos sabidores que allí havía aquel árbol de
estraña virtud. Y sabed que él no traía cavallo y ansimesmo
Maimonda palafrén mas ambos a dos cavalgavan en unas bestias de
estrañas fechuras y la en que Camilote cavalgava era más brava mas
él la amansava y era tal que parecía más mula que cavallo en la
çaguera salvo que tenía la cabeça ancha y (y) redonda a manera
de león y era muy ligera en el correr y en esta tal entendía él de
fazer su batalla.